Penguin Handbooks
The Pleasure of Vegetables

Elisabeth Ayrton was born in Surrey in 1910 and educated at
Newnham College, Cambridge, where she read English and
archaeology. She has published four novels, a book on Doric
temples and five previous cookery books, *Good Simple Cookery*,
Time is of the Essence, *Royal Favourites*, *The Cookery of England*
(a Penguin Handbook) and *English Provincial Cookery*. Since
the death of her husband, Michael Ayrton, the painter and
sculptor, she has lived in Gloucestershire, where she has a
large and beloved vegetable garden and first began thinking
about this book.

ELISABETH AYRTON

The Pleasure of Vegetables

PENGUIN BOOKS

Penguin Books Ltd, Harmondsworth, Middlesex, England
Viking Penguin Inc., 40 West 23rd Street, New York, New York 10010, U.S.A.
Penguin Books Australia Ltd, Ringwood, Victoria, Australia
Penguin Books Canada Ltd, 2801 John Street, Markham, Ontario, Canada L3R 1B4
Penguin Books (N.Z.) Ltd, 182-190 Wairau Road, Auckland 10, New Zealand

First published by Allen Lane 1983
Published in Penguin Books 1984

Made and printed in Great Britain by
Hazell Watson & Viney Limited,
Member of the BPCC Group,
Aylesbury, Bucks

Contents

Introduction

In this day when everyone is concerned about natural resources, worrying about wasting them and anxious to conserve them, it seems to me that we waste our vegetables by cooking them carelessly, serving them boringly, and thinking of them only as accompaniments to meat, poultry or fish.

This book is intended to promote and honour vegetables. They are regarded by most people as a necessary part of a proper meal, and their colours make our plates look more appetizing, but that is about all. We rarely make them into delicious dishes, grand or simple, which become specialities in the household and gourmet surprises to guests. Asparagus, mushrooms and globe artichokes, very fresh young peas and French beans are the only vegetables which many people hold in anything like the same respect as they do salmon or steak or a fine duck. In reality there are dozens of other vegetables, cheap to grow or to buy, which can be just as delicious, but there is a kind of conspiracy against the interesting cooking of cabbage, carrots, broccoli and so on. Every cook and housewife knows that, if young, they are very good boiled gently till just tender and served well drained with a little butter, and she faithfully serves them like this. But surely she must also know that if they are a little older they can be superb served in different combinations, with sauces or purées, on toast, with croûtons, gratinée, with pastry or rice, with eggs, cheese or stock.

Everyone knows this in theory and very few people put it into practice, even if they are growing their own vegetables with a great deal of care and labour. Why? It isn't just the extra time and trouble. It is rather that the English tradition is believed to be that a certain meat, fish or poultry dish is served and the vegetables, unless it is a form of casserole when some may be cooked as part of it, are accompaniments. We don't experiment with vegetables. We generally make simple mixed salads, rather than interesting and unusual ones. We have begun to use more herbs in recent years, but often do not trouble to sprinkle basil on tomato salad, add mint butter to young peas or a mixture of fresh herbs to a green salad, even though we may flavour roast chicken with tarragon or fish with parsley and fennel.

We grow a range of very fine quality vegetables in this country, and we import others from all over the world. This decade calls for a measured stringency in food as in everything else, and I hope to show that we can revive the traditions of our forefathers in serving vegetables so that they play their proper and honourable part in our cookery.

Those of us who are in a position to grow even a few vegetables should surely do so. But if we must buy all our vegetables, we can choose them carefully, and increasing numbers of us can freeze them when they are at their best and cheapest. The recipes in this book suggest combining vegetables which seem to enhance each other's flavours if cooked together, whether to constitute a main dish in themselves or to serve as an accompaniment.

The style of cookery suggested here bears little relation to that produced by certain French chefs in recent years and known variously as Cuisine Minceur, Cuisine Maigre and Cuisine Nouvelle. The first two were intended for weight and health watchers. This is not the primary intention of this book, though I believe that most of it may be helpful to both. The last, as Egon Ronay has pointed out, is not truly new but a development in the long tradition of French cookery, a development brought about by a general consciousness of the dangers of rich, heavy food and the guilt of the realization that half the world cannot eat even at subsistence level. This book contains a selection of traditional recipes, all of which have had some standing in the cooking of England and her colonies (and a few from France, Italy and Spain) in the past, and which seem particularly suitable to the present. These dishes share with the Cuisine Nouvelle an extensive use of vegetable purées to replace rich sauces, and this is ironic because purées have a long tradition in England, though neither in England nor elsewhere in Europe have they been much used in conjunction with other vegetables, or with eggs and pastry. I have for some time been collecting and trying recipes which employ such combinations. They use puréed vegetables as sauces and fillings, sometimes for other vegetables and sometimes for meat or fish. Purées nowadays are not time-consuming to make because we have blenders and food-mills, unlike our ancestors. They are cheap because, for a purée, old peas or beans can be used, and large quantities can be made when the vegetable is in season and the resulting purée frozen in small containers for use as required. A purée can be made into a rich sauce by the addition of butter and cream, but is in general even better served simply seasoned with salt and pepper and sometimes a few finely chopped herbs, so that its own flavour can be appreciated both separately and in conjunction with the flavours of the rest of the dish. For health and economy as well as subtle taste, a simple purée is often better than a rich sauce.

Looking anew at our cooking suggests that a change in the shape of the meals we serve might be a revolutionary advantage, particularly when entertaining, or on special occasions. Many recipes require a few minutes of final preparation and should then be served immediately. Traditionally we offer a starting course, often cold, and if we then have to finish the cooking of the main course, the waiting time is too long and the single-handed cook may well be hot and hurried when she serves it. A far more rational design for the small dinner party of today is to start immediately with the main course, follow it with a sweet course, ready and waiting in the oven or refrigerator, and, on special occasions, end the meal with a savoury, which can be made at the table or in the kitchen in 3–5 minutes. The rhythm of the meal is much less disturbed by the cook's activity at this point than it is before the main course.

Because there are few references to vegetables in early cookery books or in the detailed descriptions of great feasts which have come down to us, there has, until recently, been a belief that they were little considered. This is not so. Vegetables in season were taken for granted as side dishes set on the great tables, and were also often an essential part of the more elaborate dishes produced. 'Boiled Beef with Carrots', 'Duck with Green Peas', 'A Dish of Mutton with Collyflowers', 'Rabbit Smother'd with Onions', 'Veal with Hartichokes', 'Mutton Pie with Turnips and Apple' and 'Herb Pie' are all mentioned as early as the seventeenth century.

William Harrison, who in 1577 wrote a 'Description of England in Shakespear's Youthe', says that vegetables were plentifully grown and used until the time of Henry IV and then rather neglected until the early sixteenth century.

'Whereas,' he continues, 'in my time, their use is not only resumed among the poor commons, I mean of melons, pompons [a kind of gourd], cucumbers, radishes, skirrets, parsnips, carrots, cabbages, naves [field cabbage], turnips and all kinds of salad herbs but also fed upon as dainty dishes at the tables of delicate merchants, gentlemen and the nobility, who make their provision yearly from new seeds out of strange countries, from whence they may have them abundantly.'

To the poor cottagers, vegetables were all important. Their cooking would have been of the simplest. 'Pot herbs' – that is, onions, carrots, turnips, swedes or parsnips – went into the iron pot which hung over the fire, with whatever meat was available. If there was no meat, there might be stock left in the pot to improve their flavour; if there was no stock, they had to be plunged into salted water, if there was salt, which in some parts of the country was in short supply and expensive. There is an old Cornish saying: 'If the meat for the pot be short, put plenty of pot herbs: if the pot herbs be short, put plenty of salt in the water.' In Cornwall, this would probably have been sea salt. Kale and cabbage were flung in when the 'pottage' was nearly ready. Any surplus of pot herbs was stored for the dreaded winter, and peas and beans were specially grown to be dried and stored. Winter pottages often contained a small piece of bacon from the pig most cottagers kept, with dried peas and beans and perhaps an onion from the strings hung from the rafters.

Piers Plowman, in Langland's poem of the fourteenth century, says that he has no penny (with which he would buy pullets for their eggs) nor geese nor pigs nor eggs nor bacon. All he has for his family is:

> . . . two fresh cheese
> A few curds and whey,
> And an oat cake
> And two loaves of beans and bran
> Baked for my infants . . .
> However I have parsley and leeks
> And many cabbage plants . . .

The parsley, leeks and cabbage would have been boiled as a pottage over the fire. He also had milk for his 'infants', since he had a cow and calf. On this food, he hoped to be able to live until Lammastide, 1 August, when he hoped to have his harvest in.

Vegetables such as skirrets (a kind of thistle), marrows or young cabbages were boiled alone and eaten with bread, and all possible salad vegetables were eaten with cheese and bread. Not an inch of a cottage garden was wasted: flowers were grown round edges and in odd corners, but seldom for pleasure only – marigold and borage petals were scattered on soups, and gillyflowers and roses, lavender and rosemary and many others were necessities for medicines, lotions and ointments.

As many vegetables and herbs as possible were served raw as salads, both in the great houses and in the cottages. Harrison tells us that the first dish served at the evening meal throughout the summer was always a salad. The great bowls of leaves and herbs were brought in before the main dishes. Wild plants were carefully gathered: sorrel leaves, young dandelion leaves, sharp-tasting wood sorrel, mint and peppermint, tiny buds from hawthorn branches, watercress and young nettles were all carefully picked and gratefully eaten by all who had come through the long winter eating mostly dried and salted foods.

There is no doubt that spring meant even more to our ancestors than it means to us. The longing for fresh foods, for new tender leaves and shoots instead of the tough winter kale, for young rabbits and pigeons, always eaten in quantity at the end of Lent, whether from the warrens and the dovecotes of the wealthy or poached from the fields by the poor, was very great. Gervase Markham, writing in 1615, considers salads most important at great feasts and at the tables of princes. He describes them as 'simple' and 'compound' and includes 'boiled sallets', which were cooked vegetables mixed with currants, sultanas, herbs and seasoning and served cold. It must be remembered that many dishes which we would assume to have been served hot must have been eaten tepid or quite cold by all except those of the highest rank, to whom they were served first, and for them the ritual of washing the hands, receiving a napkin and, in some cases, having dishes tasted and roasts carved, allowed plenty of time for the steaming food to chill.

Many salads contained flowers, such as nasturtiums, violets and rose petals, borage and marigolds, arranged on a bed of green in the form of a house, a ship, a coat of arms. These decorative salads were seasoned and dressed and were intended to be eaten as well as looked at. Grand salads were often very elaborate indeed, and recipes for some of them are included in this book. It is interesting that they are very near to the American and Scandinavian 'compound' salads of today.

Some eighty years later than Markham, salads had become so important that the great diarist John Evelyn wrote a treatise on them, calling it 'Acetaria'. He suggests no less than seventy-two herbs and vegetables which were easily obtainable, and includes a receipt for a very elaborate dressing including yolks of hard-boiled eggs, to which he gives the charming name 'Oxoleon'. It is interesting to remember that tomatoes, which are included as a matter of course in most mixed salads today, were introduced in the sixteenth century but were not readily accepted as wholesome and, but for beets and radishes, all salads were green. This is a good principle. A carefully prepared tomato salad, dressed with salt and pepper and a little sugar and sprinkled with basil, and a green salad served separately with a good French dressing are far better than a sliced or quartered tomato added to a bowl of lettuce and watercress. The same is true of cucumber, which should be sprinkled with salt, drained and served plain or sprinkled with sesame seeds, the thin slices ranked in a long line on a cucumber dish.

A great change and development in the growing of vegetables in England began in the seventeenth century. The city of London was developing and spreading very rapidly, and in the home counties market gardening began to be recognized as a way of making a reasonable living. A countryman with extra garden space could improve his way of life by growing more of certain vegetables than his family could eat, and sending or taking them to the London markets.

In this century, Dutch gardeners settled in several areas near London and brought in the use of the hoe, an implement not previously seen in England. They are said to have brought over seed as well, and to have produced various vegetables which the English had not previously grown. From this time, the growing of good and unusual vegetables became fashionable among the gentry. In cottage gardens, where the growing of vegetables had been recognized as a necessity, the produce was often sadly poor. In 1742, in a treatise on economics, Sir Richard Weston says that in the North and West of England the growing of vegetables and the use of the hoe were scarcely known, and adds: 'In which places a few gardeners might have saved the lives of many poor people who starved these last dear years.'

Not until the eighteenth century was the potato, indispensable in England ever since, accepted and widely grown.

Many a noble and wealthy landowner took a deep interest in making beautiful, walled kitchen gardens, as well as in the planting of trees in his park and the making of pleasure gardens. Landowners all over the country, but particularly near London, began to notice each other's gardens and to arrange the exchange of special seeds or young trees with each other, sending their head gardeners on these errands. Nursery gardens, specializing in rare fruit trees, grew up around London. Leonard Gurl's Whitechapel garden was the place for the fashionable dwarf fruit trees; Rickett's had a nursery famous for fruit trees, fine shrubs and lilies, and Landon, helped by the Woburn head gardener, who was a friend of his, started a nursery at Brompton Gardens, considered by John Evelyn to be the greatest he had seen anywhere.

Perhaps the most interesting example of this new feeling in the seventeenth and eighteenth centuries for gardens, and for the fruit and vegetables that could be grown for the table, is the making of the gardens at Woburn Abbey by the fourth and fifth Earls of Bedford. The Woburn archives provide a great deal of detailed information both from accounts and references in letters, and it is clear that the large and noble household, although the high table was always served with vast dishes of meat and birds and great platters of fish on fast days, expected a wide variety of vegetables which were often served as an integral part of the main dishes. Ancient gardens at Woburn Abbey had been made by the monks to whom the Abbey had belonged until the dissolution of the monasteries in 1539, but had hardly been kept up. Almost no work on park or gardens had been done by the first Earl. The second Earl had sometimes stayed at Woburn and had been obliged, since she demanded it, to receive Queen Elizabeth I on Progress there, although the house and grounds were not in fit condition and furniture, tapestries and kitchen equipment had to be brought on wagons from the Earl's London house.

The third Earl neglected house and gardens completely, but his son and grandson rebuilt the house, first consulting Inigo Jones as architect and then devotedly laying out gardens and orchards. From this time on, plants and seeds were often bought in the London markets by the gardener of the Earl's London house in the Strand and sent to Woburn. In later years, the Woburn gardener usually ordered direct. The earliest account preserved in the Woburn papers specifically for the kitchen garden is for 1657.

For 5 Flemish Cherry Trees
For 1 May Cherry Tree
For new onion seed 1 pound.
For 1 peck sandish peas
For 1 ounce purslane seed
For 8 ounces Radish seed
For 1 ounce sweet marjoram seed
For ½ ounce of endive seed.

In 1663, John Field, a gardener of great ability and a man held in high affection by all the Earl's children, who almost always referred to him in correspondence as 'dear John Field', took over the Woburn gardens. Several of his orders for the kitchen garden are preserved, and those running through the seasons from 1675 to 1680 show that a great variety of vegetables were grown. As well as all those in the previous list, the following were ordered:

Short cucumber seed
Long cucumber seed
Parsnip seed
Red beet seed
Cabbage lettuce seed
Best orange carrot seed
Leek seed
Celery seed
Scarlet beans
Strasburg onions.
Egg peas.
Cardus seed
Salsify seed
Sweet basil
Summer savory
Rounceval peas
Artichoke plants.

A further order in 1690 shows:

A bushel of beans
Barnes' peas
Spanish onions
Spinach
Cauliflower
Savoy
Curled endive
Two dozen double mats to cover my melons.

If we consider cookery books of around the same period, for example Gervase Markham's *The English Housewife* (1640); Patrick Lamb's *Royal Cookery or the Complete Court Cook* (1710); *The Closet of the Eminently Learned Sir Kenelm Digby Knight Opened* (1669); Robert May's *The Accomplish't Cook* (1671), or later, Mrs Hannah Glasse's *The Art of Cookery Made Plain and Easy* (1747), we can find recipes for some of the dishes, fit for a nobleman's table, for which these vegetables would be required in their different seasons. The fifth Earl of Bedford might have been served with the following dishes, the vegetables, of course, depending on the season and the dinner set out in two or three 'courses', the dishes of the second course being rather lighter than those of the first. The third course, the 'Banquet', consisted only of sweet dishes and fruit and was often served to the noble host, his family and his highest ranking guests in a separate chamber, or even in a separate building erected for the purpose, small, ornate and known as a 'Banqueting House'. The first two courses might well have comprised:

A Batalia Pie
  (There are several recipes extant, but typically, its 'coffin' of pastry would have contained 3 or 4 pigeons, 4 ox palates, 6 lambs' stones, 6 veal sweetbreads, about 20 coxcombs, 4 artichoke bottoms, a pint of oysters, marrow from 3 or 4 large bones, butter, gravy, lemons, mace and seasoning. Here, vegetables play a small part, only artichokes being called for.)

Ragoo of Veal
  (Which contained onions, herbs, carrots, broad beans or young peas.)
or
Bombarded Veal
  (With green onions, herbs, artichokes and mushrooms.)

A Salamongundy
  (more usually spelt Salamagundy)
  (Mrs Glasse's recipe contains lettuce, parsley, small white onions, whole cooked French beans and white grapes.)

Mutton Stewed in Broth with turnips
Boiled Leg of Pork with Cabbages and Parsnips
Stuffed Cucumbers
  (A side dish.)
Green Peas in Cream
  (A side dish.)

A Delma
(Its name is clearly an anglicized version of the Greek 'dolmadis': stuffed vine or cabbage leaves as given in Mrs Anne Blencowe's receipt of 1694.)

Asparagus
(This was served to the Earl whenever it was available. Curiously, for many years it does not seem to have been grown at Woburn, and there are several recorded purchases.)

A Herbolace
(An omelette for meatless days, fried on both sides, containing many herbs, spinach and lettuce, all very finely chopped.)

A Green Tart
(Also for meatless days. It was made with herbs, spinach, or young green cabbage, lettuce and sometimes peas or chopped asparagus or green beans.)

Olla Podrida
(Originally a Spanish recipe, introduced to please Katharine of Aragon, this became very popular for the tables of English noblemen. Robert May in *The Accomplish't Cook* (1671) includes carrots, turnips, onions, sweet herbs, 'Cabbidge', spinach, sorrel, borage, endive, marigolds, artichokes, chestnuts and cauliflowers. He suggests using beetroots, potatoes (probably sweet potatoes at this date), skirrets, pistachios, pine kernels or pomegranate seeds to give the Olla a different flavour. May's recipe is for an enormous dish, which must have been served on several vast platters, since the meat content he suggests is a rump of beef, 4 tongues, Bologna sausages, mutton, venison, pork and bacon, all cut about 'as big as duck eggs', a goose or turkey, 2 capons, 2 ducks, 2 pheasants, 2 widgeon, 4 partridges, 4 stock doves, 4 teal, 8 snipe, 2 dozen quail and 4 dozen larks. The birds would be stewed whole, being put into the pot according to the cooking time they would need.

The finished dishes were arranged in layers, the meat first, the sausages and 'roots' on it, then the birds. The broth was then poured over and the cauliflowers, artichokes and various nuts arranged on top. The dish (or dishes) were decorated with red beetroots and sliced lemons and 'beaten butter' poured over all. It is hard to believe it would have come very hot to the table.)

Patrick Lamb, head cook to four reigning monarchs, gives a recipe for a noble dish known as Pulpatoon, later often shortened to

Pupton, which might well have been served at Woburn. It consisted of young pigeons or other birds cooked with onions, mushrooms and chestnuts, covered with a very strong 'ragoo' and then sealed into a tall, round pie of forcemeat, made with fine white bread-crumbs and plenty of herbs. It was turned out on a pewter or silver dish so that it looked like a brown loaf. Orange juice was squeezed over it and it was garnished with fried parsley.

For a fast-day dinner, dried and salted ling was cooked so that it was 'yellow as a gold noble'. The ling (which was a kind of long cod) was cooked with onions, oatmeal, carrots, parsnips and green herbs in a strong fish broth, deeply coloured with saffron. A Great Pie of Ling contained the flaked fish mixed with chopped green herbs and breadcrumbs and the yolks of a dozen hard-boiled eggs, laid in a pastry coffin with so much butter that all this would swim. The lid was made with a hole in the centre, through which a sauce of grape juice, butter, sugar and cinnamon, boiled together, was poured when the pie was nearly cooked. The lid was covered with the same sauce, and then scraped over with sugar. This was considered by Markham a very special Lenten dish.

Mrs Glasse describes a famous dish of chickens with sheep's tongues and cauliflowers. Spinach tarts and leeks cooked in wine, partridges stewed with cabbage, and always one or more great roasts and several large platters of birds (in the case of Woburn often sent up from the Earl's estate in East Anglia) would, at one time or another, have been set before the fourth and fifth Earls of Woburn.

The fifth Earl, and his father before him, both considered fruit of the greatest importance, and Woburn became famous for its orchards, some of which contained small enclosures for special fruits. Until the middle of the seventeenth century, Woburn had had two cherry orchards, and only a small number of other fruit trees and of wall fruit. In and after 1671, however, all the newer varieties of orchard fruits were most carefully collected from the stocks of various well-known gardens.

A list of the trees selected by Gilbanks, the Earl's London gardener, and sent to Woburn in 1671 reads:

45 pear trees   1/6 each
6 cherry trees
3 plum trees
60 pear trees of several sorts, grafted on quince stocks
100 dwarf cherry trees of different kinds

20 dwarf apple trees of sundry sorts
10 plum trees
10 apricots

Dwarf fruit trees were very highly thought of, partly as beautiful curiosities and partly because ladies could easily pick the ripe fruit as they strolled. At Woburn, the best of the dwarf fruit trees were grown around a large pond.

The names of the different varieties of fruit trees, dwarf or of full size, are a pleasure in themselves. We read of Elruge nectarines, Provence, Verona and Venetian peaches, red Magdalen, Purpurrey and Amber peaches, Bona Magnum, White Prunella, Mussell and Violet plums, Roman and Masculine apricots, Berry du Roi and Roselean pears. Cherry dwarfs, bought in 1674, were called Dukes, Carnations, Cluster Flanders and Great Flanders.

The state rooms of Woburn open on to a terrace on the west front of the house which ends in an archway leading to the cherry orchards. Along this terrace, oranges, citrons and lemons were grown in troughs, directly under the great windows. An orangery was built in the seventeenth century, to shelter the trees in winter, but though the oranges flourished, the more delicate citrons and lemons seldom lived very long in the English climate.

In this great household of the Dukes of Bedford, many dishes of fruit were included in the third or banqueting course of formal dinners and were also set out in the private rooms of the family. Preserves and jams, pastes of quince and currants, candied or crystallized cherries, apricots and peaches, and the peel of oranges and lemons were all highly regarded and made from the home-grown fruit in pantries and stillrooms, where ten years earlier such delicacies had been bought in London, or even sent over from France.

It is known from the Woburn family papers that the fifth Earl and first Duke of Bedford was a great trencherman, and in spite of the pleasure he took in the Woburn kitchen gardens and orchards insisted on heavy meals, always with a great deal of meat, even though in his later years it was considered bad for his health by his physicians and his family. However, even when travelling, he ordered vegetables and salads, as can be seen from the existing bills for two dinners he gave at the Red Lion in Cambridge on consecutive days in 1689. Each consisted of two courses. For the first course on 15 October, he had:

A large pike with all sorts of fish about it, a sirloin of beef, a pasty, mutton, geese, capons and sausages, a ham with 8 chickens and cauliflowers, a fricassee of rabbits and chickens, 'salading' and a dish of mince pies.

For the second course, he had:

All sorts of wildfowl, a brace of pheasants and of curlews and partridge, a dish of fat chickens and pigeons, a dish of 'all sorts of pickle and collared eals', a jowl of sturgeon, a dish of tarts and a dish of fruit.

That was one dinner. The next day he had carp instead of pike, veal and mutton instead of the sirloin of beef, a dish of tongues, udders and marrow-bones garnished with cauliflowers and spinach, geese, calf's head and sweetbreads, turkeys, collared pig, oysters and a grand salad, which in East Anglia, where it grew plentifully in the fen country, would probably have included marsh samphire, considered a royal delicacy. The second course on this day included wild fowl, sturgeon, chickens, rabbits, oysters, anchovies and tongues, snipe and larks. There was a Westphalian ham (the Earl was fond of Westphalian hams and ordered several sent direct to Woburn on more than one occasion). There were tarts and whipped syllabubs, a dish of artichokes and a salamagundy.

The first day's dinner and a simple supper cost £15 3s. 6d., the second day's, without supper, £18 11s. 6d.; vast sums even for a noble earl to spend on food alone at that time, but the Earl had business in Trinity College, and many friends there, so the dinners would no doubt have been set before the Master or the Dean and many other guests and were well suited, not only to his appetite, but to the state expected of him. Travelling in state, as he generally did to Cambridge, the Earl had music, harps, trumpets and bells, playing all through the journey, and music was provided, and charged for, at both dinners.

Such dinners, and those set before him at his orders at Woburn, were considered by his doctors and his beloved daughter, Lady Diana, as too much 'for his digestion and his blood'. The fine vegetables from his gardens, of which he was proud, only enhanced the flavour of meat and birds, and throughout his life he continued to eat as much meat as he had always done.

It is clear that from the poor ploughman to the noble Earl, vegetables were prized and carefully grown. They were also carefully cooked in the great kitchens of palace and castle, abbey and manor, for there was no lack of kitchen labour, and badly cooked food would not have been tolerated at the high table, even if it had passed by the all-seeing eye of the head cook. In the cottages, boiled in an iron pot over the open fire, vegetables were, no doubt, sometimes over-boiled, or sometimes half raw; sometimes salt was lacking, and sometimes they had to be eaten without meat, cheese, butter or even accompanying bread, but they were so welcome as hot and filling food that they must always have seemed well-cooked to those who had to eat them.

It was the Industrial Revolution and the resulting urbanization which ruined both the presentation and the reputation of vegetables in English cookery. The Duchess and the Countess still employed their head cooks or their French chefs, but with the rise of the middle class in the early nineteenth century, women who would have cooked carefully and well and spent much of their time in their kitchens became ladies and moved upstairs into their drawing-rooms, where they passed their time with less useful occupations, indifferently performed.

They could not afford the highest wages, and their cooks and kitchen maids were generally over-worked and under-trained. In general, meat and poultry were accorded a little more respect than the vegetables, which became an edible duty, rather than a pleasure. Many a child wept over the enforced eating of brown and watery cabbage, many a hungry lodger could almost have wept over his landlady's soggy, grey boiled potatoes or lumpy mashed. The lady of the house had moved out of her kitchen and we, who have returned to ours, can hardly imagine what vegetable horrors were served up to the family by the long-gone Cook General or Maid-of-all-Work.

This book is not advocating a vegetarian diet. The human race is omnivorous and has probably been so for 1½ million years. This ability to eat and digest both meat and vegetable foods is one of the early developments which gave us our great success as a species and our superiority over all others. Lions eat only meat, and when the hunting is very bad they may starve. Gorillas and other primates don't eat meat and don't graze, so they must live where the forest leaves, shoots and fruits they require are to be found abundantly. Only the chimpanzees, most like ourselves, and (very rarely) the baboons eat meat occasionally, but they are dependent on vegetation and as our species spreads more and more over the earth and destroys the great forests everywhere, they begin to die out.

In the last two centuries, more than a million years since the first human hunting bands roamed the plains and forests, killing animals and gathering roots and fruits and seeds, presently discovering the use of fire and beginning to cook their food, it has been suggested by several reformers that we should do better to stop eating meat altogether. On the other hand, no one has ever suggested that we should eat meat alone, with no green or vegetable food. Only Eskimos perforce have ever successfully lived like this. In fact, if we cease to eat omnivorously, we discard our birthright, an important factor in the success of our species and the development of our complicated culture.

For the last five thousand years of those 1½ million since *Homo sapiens* established himself as a distinct species of primate and began to prosper, cultivating his crops and domesticating animals, food has been more than the simple pleasure of a necessity fulfilled. Five thousand years ago in Egypt, in India and in the Sumerian city of Ur, spices were imported, food was varied and exotic fruits and vegetables from other lands were brought to the King as part of the tribute due from conquered tribes. In fact, the art of fine cooking had been born, and it has never died.

All the recipes in this book include vegetables or fruit. They are, therefore, grouped in two ways:
(1) in collections of dishes which have their main ingredient other than vegetables in common, i.e. Vegetables with Pastry; Vegetables with Rice; and
(2) in terms of an ordinary menu, i.e. Vegetable Soups, Vegetables with Fish, etc. Chapter headings are given in the Contents list on page 5. Recipes are listed on the opening page of each chapter, and these and individual vegetables can be looked up alphabetically in the index at the end of the book.

Many of the recipes are quick and simple to prepare and cook, but a few are elaborate and require time to be ungrudgingly spent on the collection and preparation of their ingredients. Preparing and arranging a grand salad or a Salamagundy, for instance, should give the cook real creative pleasure and should not be attempted by anyone tired or short of time. A friend of mine, who was a very fine cook, used to prepare a ratatouille at least twice a month in the summer because he so much enjoyed choosing the vegetables, setting them out on the table and sitting down to prepare them, de-seeding, peeling, slicing and chopping, and all the time admiring them. If one can cook even twice a year in this spirit of leisure and pleasure, one can consider oneself as celebrating the whole vegetable kingdom.

1. Purées, Stuffings and Forcemeats

VEGETABLE PURÉES

A vegetable purée is basically any vegetable, cooked, put through a blender, liquidizer or food processor, thinned with milk or stock and/or cream, and rather highly seasoned. Orange, lemon or tomato juice may be added, and two vegetables may be puréed together to give a subtler flavour or a better colour. Spices and herbs are often added. Purées are traditional in English cookery, but their use in the past was limited. They were not thought of as sauces for other vegetables or for meats, but simply as a way of serving rather old vegetables which would otherwise be stringy or hard; they were, therefore, used for soups, with the addition of stock or milk, or were served fairly solid and dry, as in pease pudding, which was eaten on its own or as a traditional accompaniment to pork or mutton.

A purée, until the widespread use of electric blenders, liquidizers and processors, involved a great deal of work. Daughters or kitchen maids rubbed the prepared and pre-cooked vegetables through fine wire or even through hair sieves, a process which might take the best part of an hour if a large quantity was required. Nowadays, to prepare a purée of almost any vegetable is a matter of two or three minutes with a blender or liquidizer after it has been cooked.

Some vegetable purées have a delicious flavour, but are too thin and watery unless thickened with potato, rice or the addition of some white sauce. This is true of turnips, asparagus, spinach, onions, or celery, for example. Other vegetables, such as peas or broad beans, produce a thick, solid purée and can be thinned with cream, milk or stock to the consistency required.

When using a blender to make a purée of peas or beans, it is necessary to sieve the result, rubbing not too hard through a fairly fine wire sieve. Otherwise the small pieces of the inner skins spoil the smoothness.

The recipes for purées which follow can be adapted by thinning with milk, cream, stock or, in some cases, wine, or thickening with potato, white sauce or rice, for use in various dishes, and references are made to them in other parts of this book. A thin vegetable purée can, of course, be used as a soup in its own right.

The greatest innovation in the use of purées has come in the last few years from France, where two great chefs, Paul Bocuse and Michel Guérard, and many others equally good but less well known, have developed a lighter cuisine, good for weight and for health in general, in which traditional sauces are replaced by purées of vegetables. Grilled or roast meat or poultry or grilled or boiled fish are delicious served with a purée of tomatoes, mushrooms or celeriac, for example, and only a small quantity of thickening is needed. A little cream or butter can be added if liked, but the plain purée, well seasoned, lends its fresh taste to the dish without such additions.

One vegetable is often delicious conservatively cooked, very well drained and served individually with a purée of another poured over it. Finely chopped carrots with a purée of spinach, white cabbage cooked with apple and sultanas with a tomato purée, or French or runner beans with mushroom purée are good examples.

A thickened vegetable purée makes a good filling for a savoury tart and, of course, is used for the basis of a soufflé.

Purées freeze well, and it is pleasant and useful, if not essential, to have several put up in small quantities in the freezer.

Purée of Broccoli, a Fine Hot Starting Course

Served in individual dishes, a purée of white or purple sprouting broccoli, sprinkled with crisp bacon, is delicious. Thin brown bread and butter should accompany it.

For 4   2 lb (1 kg) white or purple sprouting broccoli
6 rashers streaky bacon
2 tablespoons double cream
2 teaspoons lemon juice
salt and freshly ground black pepper
a little butter

Cut all the hard stems from the broccoli, wash in cold water and plunge into a saucepan containing 1 inch (2 cm) of boiling salted water. Boil until tender (about 15 minutes), then drain but do not press the water out. Put in a blender to make a fairly thick purée.

Remove the rinds from the bacon and cut it into very thin strips crossways. Fry them crisp and keep warm. Stir the cream into the purée, add the lemon juice and season highly with pepper and very lightly with salt. Butter 4 small dishes and divide the purée between them. Press down a little hollow in the middle of each and put in the crisp bacon. Serve immediately.

Purée of Brussels Sprouts with Nutmeg

Nutmeg marries so well with Brussels sprouts that this is one of the best of all vegetable purées. It is excellent served in individual dishes with crisp toast as a starting course, or with lamb chops or turkey as a delicious sauce. The flavour is best if the nutmeg is bought whole and freshly grated, but the prepared nutmeg sold in small jars is quite satisfactory. If frozen sprouts are used, the flavour is much reduced. These quantities will make 1 pint (6 dl) purée.

For 4   2½ lb (1–1½ kg) Brussels sprouts
½ pint (3 dl) chicken stock (can be made with stock cube), *or* ¼ pint (1½ dl) milk and 2 tablespoons thick cream
1 small teaspoon nutmeg
salt and freshly ground black pepper

Prepare the sprouts, drop into boiling salted water just to cover, and cook till quite tender. Pour off half the liquid and put the remainder, with the sprouts, through a blender or food mill till the resulting purée is quite smooth. It will probably be rather thick. Thin with chicken stock or milk and cream as preferred, and stir well. Add the nutmeg and stir again. Taste in case more salt or a little black pepper would improve the flavour, and serve very hot.

Purée of Carrots

For 4   1½ pints (9 dl) chicken stock (made with a stock cube)
1½ lb (¾ kg) carrots, peeled and thinly sliced
2 oz (60 g) long grain rice
2 teaspoons lemon juice
2 tablespoons double cream
sugar, salt and pepper

Bring the stock to the boil and put in the carrots and the rice. Boil quite briskly for 25 minutes, stirring occasionally. Drain, reserving the stock. Put through a blender, liquidizer or food mill. Add enough of the reserved stock to make the purée a little thicker than the consistency you require. Allow to cool for a few minutes. Stir in the lemon juice and then the cream, and season rather highly with sugar, salt and pepper.

Purée of Cauliflower

For 4–6   1 medium cauliflower
6 oz (180 g) mashed potato
1 oz (30 g) butter
3 tablespoons cream or milk
salt
1 tablespoon finely chopped parsley

Divide the cauliflower into florets and cook in boiling, salted water just to cover until tender (about 15 minutes). Strain, reserving about ½ pint (3 dl) of the cooking liquid. Put the cauliflower and the mashed potato into this liquid and put through a liquidizer or blender. Stir in the butter and the cream or milk and check the seasoning. Stir in the parsley just before serving.

Chestnut Purée

Serve rather thick with turkey legs or a prepared turkey joint, sweet corn and baked tomatoes. Serve thinned to the consistency of thick gravy with hot gammon or with roast chicken. Brussels sprouts or green cabbage balance the chestnut sauce.

For 6–8   2 lb (1 kg) chestnuts
1½ pints (6 dl) chicken stock (can be made with a stock cube)
3 oz (90 g) butter
3 tablespoons double cream
salt and freshly ground black pepper

Peel the chestnuts and remove the inner skins. Put in a saucepan, cover with the stock and simmer, covered, for 30 minutes. Put the chestnuts and their liquid through a blender or liquidizer. Return to the saucepan and stir in the butter. Finally add the cream and season with a very little salt and pepper. If too thick, thin with milk to the required consistency.

Mushroom Purée

This gives a thin purée of very good flavour.

For 4   ½ pint (3 dl) water mixed with ½ pint (3 dl) milk
1 lb (½ kg) mushrooms, finely sliced
½ teaspoon grated nutmeg
1 teaspoon salt
1 teaspoon freshly ground black pepper
1 teaspoon lemon juice

Bring the milk and water to the boil and put in the mushrooms. Season with the nutmeg, salt and pepper. Simmer gently for 15 minutes. Drain, reserving the liquid, and put through a liquidizer, blender or food mill. Stir in about half the reserved liquid. Add the lemon juice and check the seasoning.

For a thicker purée you will need the following additional ingredients:

1 oz (30 g) butter
1 oz (30 g) flour
3 tablespoons of cream, if liked

Proceed as above, but make a roux with the butter and flour, stirring in, a little at a time, the liquid remaining after the mushrooms have been put through the liquidizer. Stir till smooth and thick and just beginning to boil. Immediately add, little by little, the liquidized mushrooms, stirring till you have a smooth, thick sauce. Check the seasoning and add the cream, if this is to be used.

Onion Purée

For 6   1 pint (6 dl) milk
¼ pint (1½ dl) water
salt and pepper
1 lb (½ kg) onions, skinned and roughly chopped
2 oz (60 g) butter
2 oz (60 g) flour
½ teaspoon grated nutmeg

Mix the milk and water, add a teaspoonful of salt, and put in the onions. Bring to the boil, and simmer gently for 20 minutes or until the onions are quite tender. Stir from time to time and be careful that the milk does not boil over. When cooked, put the onions and liquid together through a blender or liquidizer. Make a roux with the butter and flour and stir the purée of onion into it little by little, allowing each addition to come to the boil. When all is amalgamated, boil for 3 minutes, stirring all the time. Add the nutmeg and check the seasoning. Thin with milk or cream if necessary.

Pease Pudding

For 4   ¼ lb (120 g) dried green peas
1 large onion
sprig each of parsley, thyme, marjoram and savory or
    a good pinch of dried sweet herbs
salt and pepper
1 oz (30 g) butter or margarine
1 tablespoon flour
¼ pint (1½ dl) milk
1 egg

Soak the peas overnight. Then put them in a saucepan with the peeled and chopped onion and enough boiling water to cover well. Boil until the peas are quite tender, then rub through a sieve or moulin. Add the herbs, finely chopped, and season with salt and pepper. Melt the butter in a saucepan, add the flour, and stir over gentle heat until it is a smooth paste. Add the milk gradually and continue stirring until it has boiled for 5 minutes. Add this sauce to the pea purée and mix thoroughly. When it has cooked a little, allow it to cool, stir in the well beaten yolk of the egg, and finally the white, beaten to a stiff froth. Turn into a greased pie-dish and bake in a moderate oven, 350°F, gas mark 4, for 15 minutes.

Purée of Peppers

For 4-6   4 large red or green peppers
3 oz (90 g) butter
2 oz (60 g) rice
1 pint (6 dl) stock (can be made with stock cubes)
3-4 tablespoons cream, if liked

Grill or bake the peppers dry for 5 minutes so that the skins can be stripped off. Remove the seeds and blanch the flesh in boiling water for 2 minutes. Drain and fry very slowly in 2 oz (60 g) of butter until soft. Meanwhile, cook the rice in the stock until very soft, then add the peppers. Put the peppers and rice through a blender or liquidizer. Return to the saucepan and stir in the remaining butter. Check the seasoning, and add the cream if this is to be used.

Purée of Spinach

For 4–6   2 lb (1 kg) fresh or 2 large packets frozen spinach
1 oz (30 g) butter
2 oz (60 g) double cream, if liked
a little milk
squeeze of lemon juice
salt and black pepper

If fresh spinach is used, tear away all the solid stalks from the leaves and wash the leaves well. Melt the butter in a heavy saucepan. Put in all the spinach, turn in the butter, cover and cook for 3 minutes. Stir uncovered for a further 2 minutes and allow to cool slightly. If frozen spinach is used, cook according to the directions.

Put the spinach into the liquidizer and when smooth, turn into a saucepan. Stir in the cream, if this is to be used. If the purée is to be served as a sauce, it will probably need 3 or 4 tablespoons of milk stirred in to thin it to a pouring consistency. Check the seasoning, and add a squeeze of lemon juice with the salt and black pepper.

Tomato Purée

For 4   1 lb (½ kg) tomatoes (imperfect or slightly overripe will do)
1 teaspoon sugar
salt and pepper
a pinch of basil
cream, milk or stock to thin the purée

Skin the tomatoes and put them, roughly chopped, in a heavy saucepan with the sugar, salt, pepper and basil and 2 tablespoons of water. Cook for 15 minutes. Put through a liquidizer or blender, and then through a sieve to free the purée from seeds and any bits of skin. Thin with cream, milk or stock to the desired consistency.

Turnip, Celeriac or Leek Purée

For 4–6   2 lb (1 kg) turnips (the turnips must be young so that they are not at all stringy), *or* celeriac, *or* leeks
2 oz (60 g) short grain rice
3 tablespoons double cream, if liked (can be replaced with milk if preferred)
salt and white pepper
2 teaspoons lemon juice for celeriac and leeks
4 teaspoons orange juice for turnips
2 tablespoons finely chopped parsley for celeriac

Wash and peel the vegetable to be used and cut in thick slices or rings. Put with the rice into boiling salted water just to cover, and boil till just tender (25–40 minutes according to the age of the vegetable). Drain, retaining half the liquid. Put the cooked vegetable into a blender or liquidizer, or through a food mill. Add the reserved cooking liquid and the cream or milk. Stir, and season well with salt and pepper and the appropriate juice or the parsley.

Dishes using Vegetable Purées

All the following dishes, for which detailed recipes are not given here, depend for interest on the use of vegetable purées.

Spinach
1. A fairly thick purée of spinach with lamb cutlets or chops and a potato savoury or baked tomatoes.
2. The same thickness of purée with poached eggs placed on it and the dish surrounded with triangles of crisp fried bread.
3. A thinner purée, carefully spooned over neat mounds of well-drained green cabbage, white cabbage cooked with apples and sultanas or mashed carrots. Serve with haricot or butter beans and rashers of bacon, fairly crisply fried.

Mushrooms
A rather thin purée poured over sprigs of cauliflower which have been cooked till just tender. Sprinkle with finely chopped walnuts and serve as a starting course or with chicken, roasted whole or in joints with a very little fresh or dried tarragon. All these flavours enhance each other.

Mushrooms and Gammon with Mushroom Purée
Cut gammon rashers into ½ inch (1 cm) strips and fry in a little butter with 8 oz (240 g) mushrooms, each cut in half. Place in a shallow dish and pour thin mushroom purée over them. Sprinkle the top with fine white breadcrumbs, dot with butter, and brown under the grill. Very good with rice.

Root Vegetables with Onion Purée
Over a dish of well-drained mixed root vegetables, cooked in large pieces (carrots, turnips, parsnips, swedes), pour about 1 pint (6 dl) of onion purée. Sprinkle thickly with grated cheese and brown under the grill. Very good served with crusty bread as a supper dish, or with grilled lamb chops or cutlets.

FRUIT PURÉES

Raspberries, Loganberries, Mulberries, Strawberries, Blackberries, are all puréed in the same way.

> 1 lb (½ kg) fruit
> 4 oz (120 g) sugar, melted in a little hot water
> 2 oz (60 g) double cream (unless the fruit is to be
> served with separate cream)

Put the fruit and melted sugar through a blender or liquidizer, and then through a strainer which is fine enough to retain the pips. Check that the purée is sweet enough and stir in the cream, if this is to be used.

Gooseberries, apples, plums, peaches, apricots and rhubarb (which for this purpose may be treated as a fruit) should all be cooked before blending or liquidizing. Apples should be peeled, and plums, peaches and apricots stoned, blanched and skinned. The fruit should then be cooked with a very little water and just enough sugar to take off extreme tartness. If the purée is to be used for apple or gooseberry sauce or as the basis of a fruit soup, very little more sweetening will be needed. If, however, the purée is to be served as a sweet, more sugar can be added according to taste. A fruit purée served as it is will be improved by the addition of cream and by crisp sponge fingers or home-made biscuits to eat with it.

STUFFINGS AND FORCEMEATS

Chestnut Stuffing

> 2 lb (1 kg) chestnuts
> ½ pint (3 dl) water
> 2 oz (60 g) softened butter
> salt and pepper

Slit the chestnuts and roast them for 20 minutes at 300°F, gas mark 2, in a pre-heated oven. Allow to cool a little, then remove the outer husk and brown inner skin. Put the chestnuts in a saucepan, just cover with water, and simmer till soft and floury. Be careful that they do not boil dry and catch. Put through a fine moulin or a blender, beat in the butter and check the seasoning.

Prune Stuffing

> 8 oz (240 g) prunes
> 8 oz (240 g) pork sausage meat
> 8 oz (240 g) fine white breadcrumbs
> 2 oz (60 g) ground almonds
> 1 large onion, skinned, chopped finely and lightly
>   fried until tender
> salt and pepper
> a little chopped sage
> pinch of grated nutmeg
> a little milk

Soak the prunes, then stew and stone them and chop roughly. Mix together the sausage meat, breadcrumbs, ground almonds and cooked onion. Season to taste with salt and pepper, adding a little sage and nutmeg. Moisten the mixture with a little milk, and work the prunes into it.

Forcemeat for General Use

 1 onion, skinned, finely chopped and lightly fried
    until tender
 4 oz (120 g) fresh breadcrumbs
 2 oz (60 g) finely shredded suet or margarine
 1 tablespoon finely chopped parsley
 rind of ½ lemon, grated
 ¼ teaspoon salt
 pepper

Put all the ingredients in a bowl and stir the egg well in to bind.

Savoury Rice Stuffing

 8 oz (240 g) cooked rice
 2 oz (60 g) cooked peas or mixed diced vegetables
 2 oz (60 g) finely chopped cooked onion
 2 teaspoons finely chopped parsley
 ½ teaspoon finely chopped thyme
 1 teaspoon finely chopped chives
 salt and pepper

Mix all the ingredients and season well. Stir in any juice and chopped pulp from the vegetable you are stuffing, according to individual recipes.

2. Soups

Soup in cold winter weather, served piping hot, spiced and seasoned, with crusty bread or toast, commands the appetite before it is even tasted. It looks good served in bowls, perhaps even better in a large tureen with a ladle and the bowls grouped round it.

Iced soup in the heat of summer, such as the splendid Spanish Gaspacho and the nasturtium-coloured tomato and orange soup, with green mint floating, tempt with their coolness, set out on a terrace or a garden table. Cold soups are best served direct in bowls and not from a tureen. They should always be sprinkled with finely chopped bright green herbs – mint, thyme, marjoram, chives or a mixture – and must be chilled, so that they strike the palate.

Many vegetable soups are, of course, based on purées which can be thinned to a proper consistency. Others are made from vegetables, served in the reduced liquid in which they were cooked, to which herbs, wine or a meat stock are added. This kind of pottage can be thickened with a roux or by cooking potatoes, dried peas, beans or lentils in it, and can have meat or chicken cooked with the vegetables and served in the soup. In the sixteenth century, Andrew Boorde, who had travelled in Europe, wrote in his *Dyetarie*: 'Pottage is not so much used in all Christendom as it is used in England.' A good 'pottage' makes an excellent main course, cheap and substantial. Thomas Tusser, in his rhymed book on farming (1557), writing about Lent, said:

> Now leeks are in season, for pottage full good
> And spareth the milch cow and purgeth the blood
> These having with peason for pottage in Lent
> Have spareth both oatmeal and bread to be spent.

If game or other good meat is used, a pottage can be a grand dish too.

A small quantity, just over ¼ pint (1½ dl), can precede a rather grand dinner of three or more courses. But a large bowl of good soup can be followed by a collection of cheeses and some fruit or by savoury toasts or a salad dish, and everyone will leave the table well satisfied.

Barley Cream Soup

For 4   2 oz (60 g) pearl barley
2 pints (1 litre) white stock
¼ pint (1½ dl) milk and ¼ pint (1½ dl) cream, *or* ½
    pint (3 dl) milk if no cream is available
seasoning
1 oz (30 g) butter
chopped parsley

Blanch the barley for a minute in boiling water, drain, then simmer in the stock for 2 hours. Pass through a fine moulin, add the milk and cream, the seasoning, and the butter in small pieces. Reheat and serve sprinkled with chopped parsley.

Chestnut Soup

For 4   1 lb (½ kg) chestnuts
1 onion, skinned and chopped
2 cloves
2 pints (1 litre) white or bone stock
a little milk
salt and pepper

Prick the chestnuts well and roast at 400°F, gas mark 6, until the shells crack. Remove the shells and inner skin, and pound the chestnuts lightly. Put into a pan with the onion, cloves and flavoured stock, and simmer for about 1½ hours until tender. Sieve without draining, add the milk and seasoning, and reheat, but do not boil. If too thick, dilute with a little more milk.

Potage Crécy

For 4   4 large carrots
2 onions
2 sticks celery

     1 turnip
     1 oz (30 g) margarine
     2 pints (1 litre) good meat or poultry stock
     ¼ lb (120 g) rice
     1 oz (30 g) ham or a ham bone
     12 peppercorns
     seasoning

Prepare and slice the vegetables, and sauté for 10 minutes with the margarine. Add the stock, rice, ham and peppercorns, and simmer for 1½–2 hours. Sieve without draining, removing the peppercorns. Add seasoning, reheat and serve.

Gaspacho

This Spanish peasant soup is splendid eaten on a hot sunny day or a sultry night. It must be properly chilled, very cold indeed. It has been served in Spain for generations, and used to be made with cold spring water, the vegetables and wine chilled by hanging them in the well or standing them in a stream. It has a curiously, almost magically refreshing quality.

For 4   8 oz (240 g) lettuce leaves, finely cut to ribbons
     4 sorrel or spinach leaves, also finely cut
     12 oz (360 g) tomatoes, blanched, skinned and
       roughly chopped
     ½ cucumber, peeled and diced
     1 medium onion or 6 spring onions, peeled and finely
       chopped
     1 large green pepper, de-seeded and finely chopped
     20 black olives, stoned and halved
     1 tablespoon finely chopped parsley
     2 teaspoons finely chopped thyme
     1 teaspoon finely chopped mint
     1 teaspoon salt
     ½ teaspoon freshly ground black pepper
     2 tablespoons good olive oil
     1½ tablespoons wine vinegar, white or red
     ¼ pint (1½ dl) dry white wine

Mix all the vegetables and herbs lightly together in a large bowl. Add the salt and pepper, pour over the oil and vinegar, and gently mix with your hand or a large spoon and fork. Put the bowl in the refrigerator for an hour or two but not much longer. In a jug, mix the wine with an equal quantity of cold water and stand this also in the refrigerator. When about to serve, pour the liquid over the vegetables and stir lightly. Ladle into large soup bowls and serve with plenty of brown bread.

Potage du Jour

This is a very simple everyday soup which is varied according to what vegetables are in season.

For 4   1 lb (½ kg) potatoes (small ones cooked whole are best)

1 lb (½ kg) carrots, cut in halves if large

2 small turnips, cut in pieces

4 small onions, cut in halves

8 oz (240 g) piece of boiling bacon

bouquet garni

seasoning

Any or all of the following:

    1 cup of shelled peas

    1 cup of shelled broad beans

    1 cup of prepared French beans

    1 cup of diced marrow or cucumber

    1 cup of quartered tomatoes

8 oz (240 g) cabbage, finely chopped

Put the root vegetables and the bacon in a heavy saucepan with the bouquet garni and seasoning. Cover with 2 pints (1 litre) of water, bring to the boil, and simmer gently for 30 minutes. Add all the other vegetables except the cabbage and simmer for another 20 minutes. Add the cabbage and simmer for 10 minutes more. Season again. Lift out the bacon and divide so that there is a piece for each place. Remove the bouquet garni. Ladle out the vegetables and soup so that each plateful contains some of every kind. Serve with crusty French bread.

Lentil Soup

For 4   8 oz (240 g) lentils

1 ham bone or rasher of fat bacon

1 blade mace
6 peppercorns
1 sprig parsley
1 stick celery
1 sliced onion
1½ pints (9 dl) water
1½ oz (45 g) butter
1½ oz (45 g) flour
1 pint (6 dl) milk
a little cream
½ teaspoon sugar
seasoning

Put the lentils, ham bone or bacon, flavourings, vegetables and water to cook until tender (2–2½ hours). Sieve without draining. Make a roux with the butter and flour, stir in the milk, then add the purée of lentils and bring to the boil. Cool slightly, add the cream and sugar, and reheat, without allowing to boil. Season and serve.

Minestrone

For 4 2 oz (60 g) margarine or dripping
2 oz (60 g) diced bacon
1 large onion
1 carrot
1 turnip
1 potato
1 celery stalk
½ small cabbage
2 large tomatoes
2 oz (60 g) peas or French beans
2 oz (60 g) rice or vermicelli
1 clove garlic
salt
basil or marjoram
parsley
3 oz (90 g) grated cheese

Melt the fat in a large saucepan, add the diced bacon and chopped onion and simmer for 5 minutes. Add 2 pints (1 litre) of water, and bring to the boil. Add the finely diced carrot, turnip, potato and celery stalk. After 10 minutes, add the shredded cabbage and the skinned, seeded, drained and chopped tomatoes. Cook for 25 minutes, then add the peas or diced French beans, and the rice or vermicelli. Allow to simmer gently for 45 minutes, skimming carefully from time to time. Pound a clove of garlic with salt, a pinch of basil or marjoram, and a pinch of chopped parsley. Add this to the soup, boil for 5 minutes, then serve very hot, with grated cheese.

Onion Soup (Brown)

This is the superb onion soup traditional in France. The bread and cheese make the soup a full meal in itself, and the final grilling and serving takes only 5 minutes if you have the cheese grated and the bread cut and toasted.

For 4   1½ lb (¾ kg) onions
2 oz (60 g) butter
2 pints (1 litre) brown or vegetable stock
1 small slice ham or bacon, chopped
salt and pepper
1 slice of white bread ¼ inch (½ cm) thick, crusts left on, for each person
4 oz (120 g) grated cheese

Peel and chop the onions finely. Melt the butter in a saucepan, add the onions and gently fry until well browned, but not crisp, then cover and cook very gently for 30 minutes. Add the stock, the ham, and a good sprinkling of pepper and salt. Cover and simmer for an hour. Serve in deep bowls in the following way. Fill each bowl with soup, but not too full. Toast the slices of bread on one side only, and lay toasted side down on each bowl of soup. Cover the bread thickly with grated cheese, stand the bowl under a hot grill till the cheese is stringy and sizzling (2 minutes), and stand the bowls in a warming drawer or cool oven till all are ready.

Orange and Tomato Soup

A rather expensive but surprising and stimulating soup for a special occasion.

For 4   juice of 6 oranges
1 lb (½ kg) tomatoes, blanched, stewed in ½ pint (3

dl) water and put through a fine food mill (a large
tin of tomatoes can be treated in the same way or a
tin of tomato juice used – the flavour varies a little,
but all are good)
juice of ½ a lemon
2 tablespoons caster sugar
salt and pepper
¼ pint (1½ dl) cheap brown sherry
1 tablespoon brandy or whisky
1 tablespoon finely chopped mint
about 40 small fried croûtons

Pour the orange juice into a saucepan and add the tomato purée and
lemon juice. Stir in the sugar and season to taste. Bring gently to
the boil, and at once add the sherry and the brandy or whisky. Stir,
boiling gently for 1 minute. Serve in bowls immediately, each
sprinkled with mint and with the croûtons served separately.

Palestine Soup

The flavour of the Jerusalem artichoke is both delicate and stimulating, and a bowl of this soup, served with grated Parmesan cheese
and croûtons, makes a good light lunch or supper with perhaps
some fruit to follow. The knobbly artichokes are difficult to peel
economically: the quantities given here allow for cutting off the
small knobbles with the peel.

For 6   2 oz (60 g) butter
3½ lb (1¾ kg) Jerusalem artichokes, peeled and kept
white in water to which lemon juice has been
added
1 lb (½ kg) potatoes, peeled and cut in 1 inch pieces
1 onion, skinned and finely chopped
¼ teaspoon garlic salt
salt and white pepper
½ pint (3 dl) milk
2 oz (60 g) double cream
1 tablespoon finely chopped parsley
2 oz (60 g) grated Parmesan cheese
plenty of small crisp croûtons

Melt the butter in a heavy saucepan and add the prepared artichokes. Cover and cook slowly for 10 minutes, turning and stirring. Add the potatoes, onion, garlic salt and ½ teaspoon each of salt and white pepper. Pour on 1½ pints (9 dl) of hot water (just off the boil) and the milk. Stir together. Cover, bring to the boil and boil briskly for 30 minutes, stirring occasionally. Put through a blender, return to the saucepan, check the seasoning and stir in the cream.

To serve, pour into bowls, spooning some of the thickest part from the bottom into each. Sprinkle parsley on to each bowl and Parmesan cheese on to the parsley. Serve the croûtons separately.

Fresh Pea Soup

For 4   1 lb (½ kg) fresh peas (shelled)
1 pint (6 dl) milk
½ oz (15 g) butter
croûtons
2 sprigs of mint
a little parsley

Cook the peas until tender in sufficient water to cover. Mash and sieve them into a purée, without draining, then add the hot milk. Add a dab of butter when serving. Serve with croûtons and chopped fresh mint and parsley. If the peas are young and not maggoty, they may be boiled unshelled and put through a moulin, pods and all.

Sorrel Soup

French sorrel grows in huge tufts of heavy green leaves in a kitchen garden, and 1 lb (½ kg) can easily be picked from two established plants, using the younger leaves from the centre of the plants. Young leaves can also be gathered from wild sorrel in spring, stripping from the tall stems as you pick. It is rarely available in shops, but this soup can be made from spinach, fresh or frozen, with some lemon juice added, as sorrel is much sharper in taste than spinach.

For 4–6   1 lb (½ kg) sorrel leaves, *or* 1 lb (½ kg) fresh or
frozen spinach and juice of ½ lemon
3 oz (90 g) butter
1 clove of garlic, crushed, if liked

> 2 sprigs of fresh thyme and parsley (or a pinch of
>   each dried)
> salt and freshly ground black pepper
> 1½ pints (9 dl) chicken stock, fresh or made with
>   stock cubes
> 2 oz (60 g) flour
> ¼ pint (1½ dl) double cream (can be omitted)
> about 40 crisply fried croûtons

Take the hard stalks from the sorrel leaves and discard. Wash the leaves. Melt 1 oz (30 g) of butter in a heavy saucepan and stir in the leaves, the garlic (if used), the thyme and the parsley, and season with salt and pepper. Cook over low heat for 5 minutes, turning the leaves from time to time. Stir in ½ pint (3 dl) of stock, and liquidize or put through a very fine food mill.

Melt the remaining butter in the same saucepan and stir in the flour to make a roux; gradually add the liquidized sorrel mixture, stirring all the time until it comes to the boil. Stir in the remaining stock and half the cream (if used). Bring to the boil again and check the seasoning. The soup can be served immediately, or cooled and refrigerated to be used later.

Serve in bowls with a spoonful of the remaining cream floating on each. Offer the croûtons separately.

Spinach Soup

For 4–6   2 large packets frozen spinach, chopped or leaf
> 2 onions, sliced
> ½ pint (3 dl) milk with 1 tablespoon of water added
> 2 oz (60 g) butter
> 2 oz (60 g) flour
> 1 pint (6 dl) chicken stock (fresh or made from stock
>   cube)
> ½ teaspoon nutmeg
> salt and black pepper
> ¼ pint (1½ dl) cream

De-frost the spinach, retaining the liquid. Boil the onions in the milk until just soft. Stir in the spinach and bring to the boil again. Put through a blender or food mill. Melt the butter in a large saucepan and stir in the flour to make a roux. Stir in the stock little by little, until just boiling. Cook for 2 minutes, then gradually stir in the spinach purée. Bring to the boil again, add the nutmeg and seasoning, stir in the cream and serve.

A little extra cream or a sprinkle of grated Parmesan cheese can be floated on each bowlful.

Tomato Bisque

For 5–6   1½ lb (¾ kg) tomatoes
1 teaspoon salt
good sprinkling of pepper
1 oz (30 g) butter
1 oz (30 g) flour
1½ pints (9 dl) milk
cupful of cream (if possible – if not, use extra milk)
chopped parsley
chopped mint
croûtons

Quarter the tomatoes, and put them in a saucepan with the salt, pepper and ½ pint (3 dl) of cold water. Cover and cook over gentle heat until they are a soft pulp, then rub them through a fine moulin. Melt the butter in the saucepan, add the flour and stir over gentle heat until it is a smooth paste; then very gradually stir in the milk, being careful to keep the mixture smooth. Boil for 2 minutes. Slowly add the tomato purée and stir until it is just coming to the boil again. Do not let it quite boil. Stir in a small cupful of cream, if possible, and serve with chopped parsley and mint sprinkled on each helping, and fried croûtons as an accompaniment.

Quick Tomato Soup or Sauce

For 4   1 large or 2 small tins tomatoes
1 chicken stock cube
¼ pint (1½ dl) double cream
1 teaspoon sugar
pinch dried basil
1 tablespoon tomato paste
salt and pepper

Put the tinned tomatoes into a blender or liquidizer, crumble in the stock cube and add the cream. Blend briefly and put in a saucepan over low heat. Stir in the sugar, basil and tomato paste, and add salt and pepper to taste. Bring to boiling point and make sure that the stock cube and tomato paste are entirely dissolved. This soup takes only 5 minutes to prepare and, served with croûtons of fried bread and a sprinkling of chopped parsley, has a subtle and delicate taste suggesting the highest quality fresh ingredients.

A very good sauce to serve with gammon can be made in exactly the same way if some of the liquid from the tomatoes is strained off before use, and ½ oz (15 g) butter is stirred in at the last moment.

Crème Vichyssoise

For 4   2 small onions
              4 leeks
              1 oz (30 g) butter
              3 large potatoes
              2 pints (1 litre) chicken consommé
              1 teaspoon salt
              1 pint (6 dl) milk
              pepper
              ½ pint (3 dl) whipped cream
              chopped chives

Slice the onions and the white part of the leeks, and fry them in the butter without allowing them to brown at all. Peel and slice the potatoes, then add them to the other vegetables with the chicken consommé and salt. Boil for 30–35 minutes. Rub the mixture through a sieve or moulin, then return it to the heat and add the milk. Season and bring to the boil. Chill, and fold in the whipped cream. Leave in the refrigerator at least 2 hours, and serve sprinkled with chopped chives.

Watercress Soup

For 4–6   1½ lbs (¾ kg) potatoes, peeled and cut roughly in 1
                  inch pieces
              1 large onion, skinned and very finely chopped
              1 pint (6 dl) milk
              2 bunches watercress, washed, with all stems and
                  discoloured leaves removed
              1½ oz (45 g) butter

salt and pepper
1 tablespoon finely chopped parsley

Boil the potatoes and the onion in 2 pints (1 litre) of salted water. When cooked (about 15 minutes), mash them into the water with a fork. Bring the milk to the boil separately and add it to the soup. Stir in the watercress and simmer for 10 minutes, stirring from time to time. When ready to serve, stir in the butter and continue stirring till melted. Check the seasoning, ladle into bowls and sprinkle each with parsley.

Pottage of Winter Vegetables

This recipe may be found in several very early cookery books, and in at least two manuscripts. It varies slightly in all of them but in essence is the same. Before the eighteenth century, the vegetables were not strained and served separately but were simply ladled out as part of the pottage. Served separately to accompany a piece of home-cooked gammon and preceded by the soup, the pottage makes a perfect evening meal for a chilly night. Serve crusty bread or potatoes baked in their jackets with it, and drink rough red wine or dry cider. The cream and turmeric give a very special flavour to this dish, and the crumbs thicken the broth a little. The use of bread for thickening was very general until the nineteenth century.

For 4–6
8 oz (240 g) dried haricot or butter beans, soaked overnight (pour boiling water over them)
8 oz (240 g) carrots, peeled and thinly sliced
8 oz (240 g) leeks, washed, outer leaves removed and cut in 1 inch (2 cm) segments
1 lb (½ kg) potatoes, peeled and sliced in ¼ inch (5 mm) slices
3 small turnips, peeled and sliced in ¼ inch (5 mm) slices
2 large onions, peeled and thinly sliced
3 sticks celery, washed and cut in 1 inch (2 cm) pieces
1 clove of garlic, crushed
2 bay leaves
1 teaspoon thyme (dried will do)
salt and black pepper

1 small firm green cabbage, outer leaves removed and
  stalk trimmed but left whole
2–2½ lb (1–1¼ kg) gammon or collar joint
3 oz (90 g) fine white breadcrumbs
1 teaspoon turmeric
¼ pint (1½ dl) double cream
1½ oz (45 g) butter in a slice
2 tablespoons finely chopped parsley

Bring 3 pints (1½ litres) of water to the boil in a very large saucepan.
Add 2 teaspoons of salt and ½ teaspoon of pepper, and all the
vegetables and herbs except the cabbage and the parsley. Bring to
the boil and simmer gently for 20 minutes. Then add the cabbage
and cook for a further half hour. Cook the gammon separately,
according to size. (If cooked in the soup, it is apt to make it greasy.)
Mix the breadcrumbs with the turmeric and sprinkle over the
bottom of a large soup tureen (or a large mixing bowl). Pour the
cream over. When the cabbage is tender, strain all the liquid over
the cream and breadcrumbs and put the vegetables on a separate
dish. Stir the crumbs and cream well into the broth. Put the cabbage
in the centre of the vegetables and cut it through with a sharp knife.
Put the pat of butter on it and sprinkle all over with the parsley.
The gammon may be carved and the slices arranged on the
vegetables around the cabbage or, of course, it can be carved at
table.

3. Vegetables with Fish and Shellfish

To enhance their natural flavours, fish and shellfish require very delicate vegetables, carefully cooked. Green peas, asparagus, seakale, French beans and cauliflower are all good vegetables to accompany fish. Mushrooms, tomatoes and peppers and a restrained amount of onion are excellent incorporated into certain fish dishes.

Some fruits enhance fish dishes with their slightly sharp flavour. Green grapes, gooseberries and apples are good, and can make a plain fish dish outstanding. Fennel, tarragon, thyme and parsley, saffron and mace are the herbs and spices which perhaps bring the best results.

Vegetable purées served as sauces produce excellent dishes, surprising because rarely served.

Cod or Haddock with Spices and Vegetables

Served with rice, this dish is outstanding.

For 4
1½ lb (¾ kg) cod or haddock fillets, fresh or frozen and thawed
2 or 3 parsley sprigs
1 tarragon sprig
1 lb (½ kg) onions, skinned and finely sliced
1 large green pepper
12 oz (360 g) tomatoes, skinned and quartered
1 tin anchovy fillets, drained and cut in halves
8 oz (240 g) frozen peas, cooked
¼ teaspoon ground ginger *or* 1 teaspoon crushed ginger root
½ teaspoon turmeric
salt and white pepper
4 oz (120 g) butter *or* 2 oz (60 g) frying oil and 2 oz (60 g) butter

1 oz (30 g) flour
1 tablespoon chopped parsley

Put the fish into 1 pint (6 dl) of salted water with the sprigs of parsley and tarragon. Bring to the boil and poach gently for 10 minutes. Fry the onions until soft but not brown, using 2 oz of the butter or oil. Finely chop the green pepper and fry for 5 minutes in the pan used for the onions.

Lift the fish from the cooking liquid, reserving the latter. Flake the fish, removing all the skin, and mix lightly with the onions, tomatoes and green pepper. Add the anchovies, peas, ginger and turmeric, and season with salt and white pepper. Turn the whole into a buttered shallow fireproof dish.

Make a roux with 1 oz (30 g) of butter and the flour, and stir the fish liquid into it until there is about ¾ pint (4½ dl) of the consistency of a fairly thick gravy. Pour this all over the fish and vegetables. Dot with the remaining 1 oz (30 g) butter, cover closely with foil, and cook in a pre-heated oven at 350°F, gas mark 4, for 30 minutes. Remove from the oven, sprinkle with the parsley and serve with white or brown rice.

Fish and Vegetable Stew

This is a very good stew, highly flavoured and yet subtle. It should be served with rice.

For 4
6 fillets frozen smoked haddock
6 fillets frozen fresh haddock
2 tablespoons cooking oil
4 oz (120 g) onions, peeled and finely sliced
8 oz (240 g) tomatoes, blanched, skinned and
   quartered
8 oz (240 g) carrots, peeled and very finely sliced
1 tablespoon tomato paste
½ teaspoon powdered saffron
½ teaspoon powdered thyme
½ teaspoon powdered marjoram
½ teaspoon turmeric
½ teaspoon black pepper
1 tablespoon finely chopped parsley

Skin all the haddock fillets, smoked and fresh, while still frozen, as the skin will pull off easily almost in one piece. Allow to defrost. Cut each fillet across into six pieces. Bring about 1 pint (6 dl) of water to the boil and gently simmer the smoked haddock in it until tender (about 10 minutes). Drain and set aside.

In a large, wide pan, heat the oil and fry the onions very gently till just beginning to brown. Add the tomatoes and the carrots and stir. Fry gently for 3 minutes, then add 1 pint (6 dl) of boiling water. Gently stir in the tomato paste, saffron, thyme, marjoram and turmeric, then lay in the pieces of fresh haddock. Simmer for 10 minutes more and add the smoked haddock. Stir gently, and add the pepper. If the stew seems at all dry, stir in a little more boiling water.

Check the seasoning and add a little salt if required (the smoked haddock usually provides enough). The fish should be partly flaked but plenty of larger pieces should remain. The liquid should be red-gold and very well-flavoured. Sprinkle with the parsley and serve immediately.

A Mixed Fry from Sea and Garden

This dish requires deep frying and takes about half an hour to prepare, but is well worth it. Serve with tartare sauce and chips if so much deep frying can be managed, or use frozen oven chips or rice and a green salad.

For 4   4 haddock fillets, about 1 lb (½ kg)
4 oz (120 g) prawns or scampi
1 cauliflower, divided into florets
2 courgettes, washed and cut in ¼ rings
1 onion, peeled and cut in quarters
2 eggs
2 oz (60 g) plain flour
salt
1 pint (6 dl) milk
cooking oil

Skin the haddock fillets and cut each across into four pieces while frozen. Allow to defrost with the prawns or scampi.

Divide the cauliflower into small florets, about 1 inch (2 cm) across. Place them in the bottom of a large saucepan, sprinkle with a little salt, and pour on boiling water just to cover. Allow to simmer for 5 minutes. They should be tender but firm. Drain and set aside. Divide the onion quarters into separate leaves.

Put the eggs into a bowl and beat well. Add the flour and salt, then add the milk a little at a time, and beat again till smooth and slightly foaming. This is a coating batter and should be about the consistency of thin cream. Spread out some kitchen paper. Dip each piece of fish and vegetable in the batter and lay it on the paper. If the scampi are already crumbed, they should not, of course, be dipped, but can be fried as they are.

Make the oil very hot in the deep fryer and first put in the onion leaves, which will need about 2 minutes. Lift out with a perforated slice on to a large flat dish and keep warm in a low oven. Put in the courgette slices, which will need about 3 minutes, and treat in the same way. The cauliflower will need about 2 minutes. The haddock pieces will need 3–4 minutes and the scampi 2 minutes only. Have all accompaniments ready and serve immediately.

Gingered Prawns and Mushrooms

Done for me by Maxine – V.9.

This is one of the easiest and most attractive hot starting dishes for a dinner party. It can be made ahead and baked just before serving. Serve with thin brown bread and butter.

For 6
12 oz (360 g) firm button mushrooms
1 teaspoon fresh ginger root, finely grated, *or* ½ teaspoon powdered ginger
4 oz (120 g) double cream
3 oz (90 g) butter
8 oz (240 g) frozen prawns, defrosted and drained
salt and white pepper
1 oz (30 g) flour
2 oz (60 g) walnuts, finely chopped
7 oz (210 g) fine white breadcrumbs

The mushrooms must be very finely sliced, almost paper thin, downwards through cap and stem. An electric slicer does this beautifully in a minute, but it can be done carefully by hand.

Stir the ginger into the cream. Melt 2½ oz (75 g) butter in a large shallow pan over low heat. Put in the mushrooms and sauté very gently for 10 minutes. They should be tender and almost transparent but not at all brown. Stir in the prawns and mix gently with the mushroom slices. Season with salt and pepper and cook for 1 minute. Stir in the flour and work it gently and evenly into the juice and butter. When it begins to boil and thicken, stir for another minute, then add the cream and work it in till just beginning to bubble.

Check the seasoning and divide among six flat individual fireproof dishes. Mix the walnuts with the crumbs and sprinkle over the tops. Put a small piece of butter on each dish, and put into a moderate oven, 350°–400°F, gas mark 5, near the top, for 7 minutes. Check after 4 minutes to make sure the tops are not becoming too dark, as walnuts brown very quickly. If so, move them lower in the oven and cover lightly with foil.

Mackerel with Gooseberry Sauce

Gooseberries are traditional with mackerel in Cornwall. The combination is very good and is best served with brown bread and butter.

For 4 4 medium sized mackerel, cleaned and split open,
       heads and tails removed
     2 tablespoons plain flour or fine oatmeal
     salt and pepper
     a little butter
     ½ pint (3 dl) gooseberry purée (see p. 33)

Rub the mackerel lightly with seasoned flour or with fine oatmeal – either is good. Grill or dry fry the fish, just greasing the skin with butter, until cooked through. Serve direct on plates with the gooseberry purée poured beside but not over the fish.

Mackerel Stuffed with Gooseberries and Served with Green Peas, Mint and Parsley

For 4 4 mackerel, cleaned, heads and tails removed and
       split open to lie flat
     2 tablespoons fine oatmeal or plain flour
     ½ pint (3 dl) gooseberries, topped, tailed and roughly
       chopped, and stewed with 2 tablespoons sugar and
       1 tablespoon water until just tender (keep hot)
     2 tablespoons finely chopped parsley

1 lb (½ kg) peas, shelled weight, fresh or frozen,
  cooked until tender
1 tablespoon finely chopped mint

Rub the mackerel with flour or oatmeal and grill or fry as in the previous recipe. Spoon the gooseberries, with as little juice as possible, on to one half of each fish and fold the other half over to form a lid. Sprinkle with parsley. Serve quickly on very hot plates, with a helping of peas sprinkled with mint.

Trout with Purée of Spinach and Almonds

This is a very pretty dish for a dinner party. Fresh English trout are best, but frozen rainbow trout can be used. The purée of spinach should cover a long, shallow fireproof dish and should be about 1½ inches (3 cm) deep. The trout, skins slightly browned and crisped, should be laid in a row on this green bed and the whole scattered with very crisp slivers of fried almonds.

For 6　　　1½ pints (9 dl) spinach purée (see p. 31)
　　　　　　6 trout, each weighing about ½ lb (240 g), cleaned
　　　　　　　　(heads and tails are generally left on but can be
　　　　　　　　removed if preferred)
　　　　　　a little flour
　　　　　　salt and freshly ground black pepper
　　　　　　3 oz (90 g) butter
　　　　　　4 oz (120 g) blanched almonds, roughly chopped
　　　　　　　　lengthways into slivers

Heat the prepared spinach purée. Rub the trout all over with seasoned flour. Melt the butter to the foaming stage in a very large pan and fry the trout for 3 minutes on each side. Pour the spinach into a large, shallow ovenproof dish and lay the trout on it in a row. Put in the oven to keep hot while frying the almonds in the butter in which the trout were cooked, turning and shaking all the time, for a minute or two. They should be a pale, golden brown. Pour them, with the butter, all over the trout and serve immediately.

Cocottes of White Fish with Mushrooms and Mushroom Purée

An excellent starting course or a light main course, served with a salad and preceded by soup. For this dish, small soufflé dishes or ramekins, or individual dishes in enamel or stainless steel, one for each person, will be required.

For 4   a little milk
4 fillets haddock, lemon sole or cod, all skin removed (if frozen, the skin will pull off easily before the fish is thawed)
salt and pepper
pinch of powdered ginger
6 oz (180 g) mushrooms, sliced and lightly sautéed in butter
½ pint (3 dl) mushroom purée (see p. 29)
2 oz (60 g) fine white breadcrumbs
1 oz (30 g) butter

Bring equal parts of milk and water just to boiling point and season with salt. Slip in the fish fillets, being careful not to break them, and poach gently until the fish is cooked (7–10 minutes). Drain very carefully. Butter the cocotte dishes and put a fish fillet in each. If the fillets are long, roll loosely and stand each roll on its side. Sprinkle with a little salt and pepper and a tiny pinch of ground ginger. Pack the sautéed mushrooms round them and fill up the dish with the purée so that the fish is just covered.

Sprinkle each dish with the crumbs and dot with butter. Put into an oven pre-heated to 350°F, gas mark 4, for 7 minutes. The purée should be just beginning to bubble and the breadcrumbs should be a light golden brown. Serve immediately.

4. Main Course Dishes: Vegetables Alone or with Meat or Chicken

This section is made up of a small collection of excellent dishes which form a main course for a good meal. Some of them are good served with plain rice, potatoes or crusty bread. Some of them stand alone.

In all these dishes the flavours and the quality and quantity of the vegetables are even more important than the meat or chicken included in some of them. Several of these recipes are particularly good if made in large quantities for a party.

None of the recipes is very quick to prepare, but all are quite easy to make and very rewarding when set before family and guests.

Assorted Vegetable Platter with Gammon and Purées

This is a recipe for a special meal rather than a simple dish. It is best for a family lunch or supper party when eight or ten people will be present. Its success depends very largely on how it is presented. The vegetables, each separately cooked, look well in separate piles on a very large platter, or in smaller, matching bowls or dishes, arranged on a tray placed in the middle of the table. The two purées which accompany them should be prepared ahead, and served in matching bowls or sauce boats, with ladles. The gammon is placed in the centre of the vegetables. It is not a dish for a formal occasion unless there is help in the kitchen, as it cannot be prepared very long before it is served and the final preparation is exacting. It is, however, splendid for family and family friends.

Choose any five or six vegetables from the following list:

For 8–10   1½ lb (¾ kg) small new potatoes, scrubbed and
                 cooked in their skins (best with parsley)
        1 lb (½ kg) shelled peas (best with mint)
        1 lb (½ kg) shelled broad beans (best with basil)

1 lb (½ kg) skinned tomatoes, cut in quarters and
baked (best with basil and rosemary)

1 lb (½ kg) topped and tailed French beans (best with
parsley)

about 1 lb (½ kg) cauliflower in florets (best with
parsley)

1 lb (½ kg) courgettes, cut in ¼ inch (½ cm) slices
(best with chives and parsley)

1½ lb (¾ kg) finely sliced Chinese leaves

1½ lb (¾ kg) finely chopped white cabbage with
apples, onions and sultanas

1 lb (½ kg) peeled and thinly sliced carrots (best with
parsley)

1 lb (½ kg) peeled turnips, cut in ½ inch (1 cm)
cubes (best with orange zest)

1½ lb (¾ kg) leeks, washed and cut in 1 inch (2 cm)
lengths (best with parsley)

2 lb (1 kg) broccoli (add a little lemon juice)

1 lb (½ kg) calabrese, divided into small heads (add a
little lemon juice)

1½ lb (¾ kg) mangetout or sugar peas, strings
removed (best with mint and parsley)

Cook the chosen vegetables separately in the usual manner until
just tender. Drain them carefully, and keep hot in a low oven in
bowls or dishes covered with foil. They should not be kept waiting
for much over half an hour.

8 gammon rashers
3 oz (90 g) butter
a little sugar
1 pint (6 dl) spinach purée (see p. 31)
1 pint (6 dl) mushroom purée (see p. 29)
prepared ahead or day before
2 tablespoons finely chopped fresh parsley
1 teaspoon powdered rosemary
2 teaspoons powdered basil
1 teaspoon chopped onion
½ teaspoon orange zest
1 tablespoon finely chopped mint

Fry the gammon rashers gently in 1 oz (30 g) of butter. Turn after 3 or 4 minutes and sprinkle the cooked sides lightly with sugar. When both sides are light brown and slightly glazed in appearance, cut each rasher into six strips with kitchen scissors, wrap in foil and keep hot with the vegetables.

Dish the vegetables, put a small piece of butter on each heap or in each bowl and sprinkle with the appropriate herbs. Pile the gammon strips on a small flat dish in the centre of the vegetables, if they are in bowls, or in the centre of the large dish on which they are heaped. Pour the boiling purées into bowls and serve immediately. Service at table must be done quickly and neatly so that the vegetables do not have time to get cold.

Bubble and Squeak

Bubble and Squeak, a traditional English peasant dish, is closely related to the Irish dish, Colcannon. Originally, Bubble and Squeak was finely chopped green cabbage with a little onion, fried fast and furiously in butter with slices of peppered, cooked, lean beef. Dr Kitchner, in his *Cook's Oracle* of 1817, says of it:

> When midst the Frying Pan in accents savage
> The beef, so surly, quarrels with the cabbage.

In later recipes, however, cooked and mashed potato was added to the cabbage and the sliced beef was cooked separately and laid round the browned cake of vegetables, so that there was nothing to 'bubble and squeak' and the dish was really Colcannon with hashed beef. The following is an acceptable recipe for the Bubble and Squeak of today.

For 4   8–12 oz (240–360 g) cooked green cabbage, savoy or
                broccoli, very well-drained and finely chopped
             1 lb (½ kg) cooked mashed potatoes, well seasoned
                and mixed with a little milk and butter
             salt and pepper
             1 large onion, peeled and finely chopped
             a little butter

Mix the cabbage and potato, seasoning highly. Using a large pan, fry the onion gently in butter until it is soft but not browned. Add it to the cabbage and potato, turn the mixture into the pan in which the onion cooked, and fry gently, shaking the pan from time to time to prevent sticking. When the mixture is browned underneath (about 15 minutes), put a plate over the pan, turn the pan upside down and remove it. Reheat the pan with a little more butter in it, slide the cake back into the pan, browned side on top, and fry until brown underneath. Slip on to a dish and serve very hot. It may be kept hot in the oven without spoiling.

French Beans and Creamed Breast of Chicken

For 4
2 lb (1 kg) French beans, ends and strings removed (frozen whole green beans can be used)
4 oz (120 g) mushrooms
2 oz (60 g) butter
½ pint (3 dl) béchamel sauce
3 chicken joints (breasts if possible), pre-roasted, all skin and bone removed and meat cut into ½ inch (1 cm) pieces
¼ pint (1½ dl) double cream
salt and freshly ground black pepper
1 tablespoon finely chopped parsley mixed with 1 teaspoon finely chopped fresh or dried tarragon

Cook the beans in boiling salted water to cover, for 15 minutes (if frozen beans are used, cook according to the directions). While they are cooking, slice the mushrooms finely and sauté in the butter. Keep warm in a low oven.

Very gently heat the béchamel sauce and when just warm, stir in all the prepared chicken. Continue to heat till boiling point is reached, stirring very frequently. Stir in half the cream and set aside, covered, to keep hot.

Drain the beans, pour the remaining cream into the saucepan, and return the beans to cook in the cream for a further 5 minutes. Season with salt and pepper. Dish up the beans on to a wide shallow dish, so that they form a ring all round it. Pour the chicken into the empty centre. Sprinkle the mushrooms all over the beans and the parsley and tarragon over the chicken. Serve with plain or saffron rice.

An Eighteenth-century Dish of Chicken with Peas

It seems likely that in the last 150 years our peas have improved in flavour and tenderness but our chickens have not. This dish was served in many well-to-do farms or manors all over the country, though the present recipe comes from Somerset. It is very good served with plain or saffron rice. Excellent for a dinner party.

For 6   1 large roasting chicken, or 6 breast portions
(defrosted if necessary)
4 oz (120 g) butter
1½ lb (¾ kg) shelled or frozen peas
1 small lettuce
3 oz (90 g) shallots or small onions, chopped very fine
salt and pepper
a little sugar
bunch of marjoram and mint with 2 or 3 sprigs of
tarragon
½ oz (15 g) flour
¼ pint (1½ dl) stock
2 tablespoons double cream
1 tablespoon parsley chopped very fine
12 triangles of crisp fried bread or puff pastry,
prepared in advance and heated while the dish
cooks

Roast the whole chicken or the joints in a little butter and while roasting, prepare the peas. In a fairly large saucepan, melt ½ oz (15 g) of butter without colouring. Add half the peas, and put the lettuce, washed and divided into leaves, and half the shallots on them. Sprinkle with salt and a little sugar and pepper, and lay the bunch of marjoram, mint and tarragon on top. Put in the remaining peas, and on top of them the rest of the shallots, and some more sugar, salt and pepper. Pour in ½ pint (3 dl) cold water. Cover closely, bring to the boil, and simmer for 20 minutes or until the peas are tender. Drain any excess water. Gently stir in the remaining butter and keep warm.

Remove all skin from the chicken and cut and pull the meat from the bone. The pieces should be about 1½–2 inches (3–4 cm) long. Remove the bunch of herbs from the peas. Stir all the chicken very gently into the peas and keep warm on a shallow dish. Pour off all the fat from the pan in which the chicken roasted. Put on a low heat, add the flour, and stir till it has taken up all the pan juices. Stir in the stock. When boiling, add the cream and stir till it boils again. Pour all over the chicken and peas, sprinkle with parsley, and arrange the croûtons round the edge of the dish.

Chicken with Winter Cabbage and Walnuts

This dish looks very good surrounded by a border of mashed potato.

For 6   3 cooked chicken joints or a small cooked chicken
3 oz (90 g) butter *or* 2 tablespoons cooking oil
2 large onions, peeled and sliced
3 lb (1½ kg) white, hard salad cabbage, finely
   shredded
8 oz (240 g) green grapes, blanched and stoned
4 oz (120 g) shelled walnuts, coarsely chopped
¼ pint (1½ dl) white wine
salt and white pepper
1 tablespoon finely chopped parsley

Strip all the meat from the chicken, discarding skin and bone. The pieces should be 1½–2 inches (3–4 cm) in length. Heat the butter or oil in a large fireproof casserole with a lid, and melt the onions in it till tender but not coloured. Stir in half the cabbage, the skinned grapes, the walnuts and the chicken pieces. Add the remaining cabbage and stir all well together. Pour over the wine and season rather highly. Cover and cook at 350°F, gas mark 4, for 1½ hours. Remove and turn on to a flat warmed dish. Sprinkle with the parsley and serve at once.

Circassian Chicken

This is a very old recipe, sometimes served as a side dish at feasts which took place in the autumn when mushrooms were available. No onions or garlic were included, so that the delicate and distinctive flavours of the mushrooms and walnuts were not masked. Serve with plain boiled rice or potatoes baked in their jackets, and a salad.

For 4–6   12 oz (360 g) mushrooms, sliced
3 oz (90 g) butter

all the meat from a 2½ lb (1¼ kg) chicken, divided
   into strips about 1 inch (2 cm) in length
4 oz (120 g) fresh brown breadcrumbs
¼ teaspoon mace
¼ teaspoon turmeric
8 oz (240 g) walnuts, finely chopped
salt and freshly ground black pepper
2 oz (60 g) walnuts, coarsely broken

Lightly fry the mushrooms in the butter. When they are beginning
to soften, add the chicken pieces and fry gently for 5 minutes,
turning and stirring all the time. Add the breadcrumbs, mace and
turmeric and stir for a further minute, then add the finely chopped
walnuts and the seasoning. Stir and fry for 2 minutes. Turn into a
shallow warmed serving dish with all the pan juices, sprinkle with
the coarsely chopped walnuts, and serve very hot. The dish can be
kept hot in the oven for 20 minutes or so without drying or spoiling
the delicate flavour.

Curried Cabbage with Hard-boiled Eggs

This recipe from Asia is, to us, a very unusual way of treating
cabbage. It is delicious served with plain boiled rice.

For 4   4 hard-boiled eggs
             2 lb (1 kg) green or savoy cabbage
             1 large onion
             1 oz (30 g) butter
             1 teaspoon chili powder
             ½ teaspoon turmeric
             salt and pepper
             2 oz (60 g) desiccated coconut (or flaked or chopped
                almonds, if preferred)

Halve the hard-boiled eggs and arrange in a shallow, fireproof dish
big enough to take the vegetables.

   Cut the hard stalk and any tough outside leaves from the cabbage
and shred it very finely. A food processor does this admirably. Peel
the onion, slice very finely, and fry till just soft in the butter. It should
not colour at all. Rinse a heavy saucepan with water and put in the
cabbage, mixed with the onion and the butter in which it fried, the
chili powder and the turmeric, ½ teaspoon of salt and a good pinch of

black pepper. Cover and cook on fast heat, stirring from time to time until there is enough moisture from the vegetables to prevent them sticking. Then cook for a further 5 minutes, covered, without stirring. Check the seasoning, and test the cabbage which should be slightly crisp. Add the coconut or almonds and stir continually for 2 or 3 minutes. Pour over the eggs and serve with plain boiled rice.

Gammon Gratinée with Eggs and Beans

This dish can be varied by using different vegetables, and made more substantial by adding a ring of creamed or small new potatoes round the edge of the dish. It is best of all when the peas or beans can be picked from the garden and cooked immediately, but it is quick to prepare and still very good with frozen ones.

For 4 1 lb (½ kg) shelled or frozen peas or broad beans
4 gammon steaks
3 oz (90 g) butter
2 oz (60 g) fine white breadcrumbs
a little finely chopped mint for peas, or a little finely chopped marjoram for beans
4 eggs, well beaten and seasoned with salt and freshly ground black pepper

Boil the peas or beans till just tender. While they are cooking, cut the gammon steaks into strips about ¼ inch (½ cm) wide and 1½ inches (3 cm) long. Fry them lightly in 2 oz (60 g) of butter until they are slightly browned and glazed. Drain the peas or beans and keep warm. Lift the gammon strips and keep warm on a separate dish. Put the breadcrumbs into the pan in which the gammon cooked and fry lightly, shaking and turning all the time. When light golden brown, turn the gammon back on to the crumbs and shake so that crumbs adhere to all the strips.

Dish the peas or beans to form a rough circle on a flat dish, and pour the gammon and the crumbs into the centre. Sprinkle the peas or beans with half the finely chopped herbs, and keep warm while you lightly scramble the eggs, using the remaining 1 oz (30 g) of butter. Spoon the eggs (which should be only just setting) on to the gammon, sprinkle with the rest of the mint or marjoram, and serve immediately.

Gammon and Red Cabbage Cooked in Wine

In this excellent supper dish, almost all the wine and stock are absorbed as the dish cooks.

For 4   ¼ pint (1½ dl) stock (may be made up from beef
         stock cube)
      ¾ pint (4½ dl) red wine
      2½ lb (1¼ kg) red cabbage
      8 oz (240 g) onions, cut in rings
      1 oz (30 g) sultanas
      1 teaspoon sugar
      very little salt
      plenty of black pepper
      a little butter
      2 rashers of gammon, each about 4 oz (120 g), cut
         into strips
      16 small potatoes, peeled or scraped

Make up the stock, add the wine, and boil briskly for 3 or 4 minutes so that it reduces slightly. Meanwhile, cut the outside leaves and main stalk from the cabbage, and grate all the rest on the coarsest part of the cheese grater. Mix the onion rings and sultanas lightly into the grated cabbage, add the wine and stock and season with sugar, salt and pepper. Butter a wide, shallow, fireproof dish and put in the mixture, pressing it down to give an even surface. The liquid should come almost to the top. Cover closely with foil and bake at 350°F, gas mark 4, for one hour. Remove the foil and arrange the gammon strips all over the top. Dot with a little more butter and return to the oven for 20 minutes. Meanwhile, boil the potatoes very gently so that they remain whole. Drain well and toss in a little butter. Take the gammon and cabbage from the oven, arrange the little potatoes on top around the edge of the dish, and serve.

Haricot Pot Pie

This is a very good supper dish made in a larger quantity for an informal party. It is good served with French beans or a green salad, and brown bread and butter.

For 6	8 oz (240 g) haricot beans, soaked in boiling water overnight
	2 large onions, skinned and chopped
	2 oz (60 g) butter
	2 medium cooking apples, peeled and thinly sliced
	1 lb (½ kg) large pork sausages
	½ teaspoon turmeric
	½ teaspoon mace
	½ teaspoon dried thyme
	¾ pint (4½ dl) rough cider or red wine
	¾ pint (4½ dl) any good stock (or make with cube)
	salt and black pepper

Boil the haricot beans in fresh, salted water for 1½ hours. In the last half hour, gently fry the onions in 1½ oz (45 g) of the butter, so that they become soft and transparent but not brown. Use a large, rather shallow casserole. When the onions are almost done, add the apples and fry gently for a further 5 minutes. Stir in the spices and herbs. Drain the beans and stir in. Pour in the cider or wine and the stock. Season well, bring to the boil on top of the stove and then put in the oven pre-heated to 350°F, gas mark 4. Cook uncovered for a further 1½ hours, by which time the beans should have absorbed most of the liquid and formed a crust.

Half an hour before the casserole will be ready, fry the sausages in the remaining butter and when cooked, carefully cut each into six rings, including the ends. Place them all over the top of the casserole, so that the rings lie flat on the bean crust, and put back in the oven for the remaining few minutes.

Roast Leg of Spring Lamb with Peas

This dish can also be made with noisettes of lamb or with loin chops. Its distinctive and delicious feature is that the lamb is accompanied by a purée of peas well-flavoured with mint, and also by fresh peas cooked with small onions and tiny new potatoes. The skin of the lamb must be crisp, and each helping should be placed on the diner's hot plate with a helping of peas and another of purée placed near but not on top of it.

| *For 4* | 1½ pints (9 dl) purée of green peas |
| | 1 tablespoon very finely chopped fresh mint |

salt and freshly ground black pepper
1 small leg of lamb or 4 noisettes
a little flour
2 or 3 sprigs of rosemary
butter
24 very small new potatoes
1 lb (½ kg) peas, fresh or frozen (if the latter, *petits pois* are best)
16 button onions *or* spring onions *or* shallots
1 tablespoon very finely chopped fresh parsley

Prepare the purée, stirring in half the mint before blending and seasoning lightly. Roast the lamb in the usual manner, lightly flouring the outside to make sure that it becomes brown and crisp, and place the sprigs of rosemary on it. It should be a little pink near the bone, unless this is disliked. If noisettes are to be served, lightly fry in butter when the vegetables are ready. When the noisettes are turned, allow the rosemary to remain in the butter. It is not served.

Put the potatoes into boiling, salted water and boil for 10 minutes. Put the onions into 1½ pints (9 dl) of boiling, salted water and boil gently for 15 minutes. Add the defrosted or fresh peas and boil for a further 10 minutes for the first, and 15 minutes for the second. Drain the potatoes when cooked, and keep warm in a little butter. Drain the peas and onions, add the potatoes, and stir in the remaining mint and ½ oz (15 g) butter. Stir over heat for half a minute, check seasoning, and turn on to a serving dish. Sprinkle with parsley and keep warm while the lamb is dished.

Macaroni and Ham Loaf with Purée of Peas or Tomatoes

For 4 4 oz (120 g) quick macaroni, boiled in salted water till just tender, and well drained
4 gammon steaks, lightly fried and cut in strips about ¼ × 1 inch (½ × 2 cm)
3 oz (90 g) grated cheese
2 eggs, beaten with ¼ pint (1½ dl) milk
pepper
1 oz (30 g) butter
¾ pint (4½ dl) purée of peas or tomatoes (see p. 31)
1 tablespoon finely chopped parsley

Mix the macaroni, gammon and cheese into the beaten eggs and milk. Season well with pepper. Pour into a well-buttered soufflé dish or other straight-sided ovenproof dish and cover lightly with foil. Stand the dish in a baking tray of hot water to come about a third of the way up, and bake at 350°F, gas mark 4, for 30–40 minutes or until the mixture is firmly set.

Heat the purée and check the seasoning. Turn out the macaroni mould on to a heated dish and pour the purée all over. Sprinkle with the parsley and serve immediately. Individual green salads are good with this.

Macaroni Pie

Recipes for macaroni pie go back to the Italian Renaissance and even earlier. It was a feast day dish to be eaten *en famille* or when entertaining formally. It was also a dish made in noble and peasant houses alike, since expensive ingredients could be omitted and cheaper ones substituted without spoiling the dish. It was made as a very large dish and was often eaten first hot and then cold for a late supper. Quantities given here will serve a party of twelve, or half can be served and half frozen. The ingredients should all be bought the day before and most of them prepared and kept overnight in the refrigerator. The assembling of the dish is then a pleasant job which should take about 1½ hours, and the cooking time should be about 2 hours. A tomato salad and a green salad dressed with oil and plenty of lemon juice are the best accompaniments and dry white wine the best drink.

For 12
2 teaspoons turmeric
½ teaspoon powdered ginger
½ teaspoon mace
½ teaspoon grated nutmeg
2 cloves of garlic, well crushed
2 teaspoons finely chopped oregano
2 tablespoons spring or Welsh onions or chives, finely chopped
1½ pints (9 dl) quick tomato sauce (see p. 48)
½ pint (3 dl) dry red wine, boiled till it is reduced by half
½ pint (3 dl) cream
6 oz (180 g) butter

2 lb (1 kg) quick macaroni, cooked and rinsed under
the cold tap to wash off starch and keep the pieces
separate

4 oz (120 g) sultanas, soaked for a few minutes in hot
water

1 lb (½ kg) mushrooms, finely sliced and sautéed in
3 oz (90 g) butter

salt and freshly ground black pepper

any two

or more

of:

12 oz (360 g) small French beans, cooked till just
tender

8 oz (240 g) peas, fresh or frozen, cooked till just
tender

8 oz (240 g) carrots, diced and cooked till just tender

8 oz (240 g) young broad beans cooked till just tender

1 green pepper, de-seeded, chopped and fried till
tender

all the meat from one roast chicken, without skin or
bone, cut in strips about ¼ inch (½ cm) wide

6 gammon rashers or a small gammon joint, cooked
and cut in strips like the chicken

4 tablespoons finely grated cheese – ½ Parmesan and
½ Cheddar if possible

4 oz (120 g) almonds, coarsely chopped and fried in a
little butter till very light brown

2 tablespoons finely chopped parsley

Have ready two large ovenproof dishes, 2 or 3 inches in depth. Stir
the turmeric, ginger, mace, nutmeg, garlic, oregano and spring
onions or chives into the tomato sauce and heat very gently in a
large saucepan until almost boiling, then stir in first the wine and
then the cream.

Melt 3 oz (90 g) of butter in a very large saucepan and stir in the
macaroni, little by little, separating the pieces as you do so. Turn in
the butter for 2 or 3 minutes. Add the sultanas and mushrooms. Stir
and season well and put a level layer about 1 inch (2 cm) deep in the
bottom of each dish. Pour about a third of the sauce over the layers.
Cover with thin layers of one of your chosen vegetables, and put
over this layers of about half the chicken and ham. Repeat, using all
the vegetables and meat, but leaving enough macaroni and sauce for
the top layers. Cover with the cheese, and bake for 40 minutes in an
oven preheated to 350°F, gas mark 4.

Sprinkle the tops with the almonds and return to the oven for a further 5 minutes. The dish to be served will keep warm at a lower temperature for about half an hour, or can be made up and kept in the refrigerator for several hours before its final baking. Sprinkle the parsley over the top when about to take it to table. The second dish should be frozen as soon as it has cooled.

Supper from a July Garden

This particular combination of vegetables and herbs provides such fresh and poignant flavours and looks so appetizing that, once served, it will be asked for again. An allotment or a kitchen garden will provide all these vegetables so that, freshly dug and gathered, they are perfection, but carefully chosen from a shop they will be very good.

For 3–4   2 lb (1 kg) small new potatoes, scraped
2 oz (60 g) butter
1 lb (½ kg) young carrots, scraped and cut in ¼ inch (1 cm) rings
1 small lettuce, or some outside leaves of a large one
1 lb (½ kg) peas, fresh or frozen
2 oz (60 g) double cream
1 tablespoon finely chopped mint
4 cooked artichoke bottoms, *or* 8 oz (240 g) mushrooms, finely sliced
1 tablespoon marjoram and thyme, finely chopped
1 tablespoon finely chopped parsley
1 tablespoon finely chopped chives
salt

Put the potatoes into boiling, salted water and boil very gently till just cooked, about 20 minutes. Drain, pile in the middle of a large flat dish, put 3 or 4 pieces of butter on them and keep warm in the oven. Put the carrots in a separate saucepan of water and boil till tender, about 15–20 minutes. Put the lettuce leaves, torn into large pieces, and the peas into a third saucepan of boiling, salted water and cook until just tender, about 10 minutes. Drain, pour the cream into the hot saucepan, and put the lettuce and peas back into it. Put ½ oz (15 g) of butter on the peas, scatter with the mint, cover and keep warm.

Fry the artichoke bottoms or mushrooms lightly in 1 oz (30 g) of butter. Drain and keep warm. Drain the carrots, put in the remaining butter and add the marjoram and thyme. Put half at each end of the dish containing the potatoes. Put half the peas with all their cream and butter on each side. (The cream makes the sauce for the whole dish.) Put the artichokes or mushrooms between. Put back in the oven for 3 minutes so that all will be very hot. Sprinkle the parsley and chives all over the vegetables before serving.

The White, the Red and the Green

(Chicken fillets with tarragon, served on purées of spinach and carrots)

The four flavours of this dish are as elegant as the three contrasting colours. Serve on a large, shallow ovenproof dish, with French bread and unsalted butter.

For 6
1 lb (½ kg) spinach purée (see p. 31)
1 lb (½ kg) carrot purée (see p. 27)
6 chicken joints (wing and breast)
1 small onion, skinned and very finely chopped
salt and pepper
4 sprigs fresh tarragon or 3 teaspoons dried
juice of 1 lemon
2 oz (60 g) cooking oil
3 oz (90 g) fine white breadcrumbs

Prepare the spinach and carrot purées. Set aside and gently re-heat just before assembling the dish.

Remove the chicken meat from the bones, using scissors and a sharp pointed knife. It should be possible to cut two or three fairly large fillets from each joint. (Reserve the bones for stock.) Lay the chicken fillets on a large plate and sprinkle lightly with the onion, salt and pepper and about half the tarragon. Pour a little lemon juice on each and then the oil, and leave to marinate for about an hour, or longer if preferred.

Pour off the marinade into a frying pan and very gently fry the chicken fillets, turning several times. When just done (about 6 minutes) sprinkle the breadcrumbs and the rest of the tarragon over them and turn once more. Heat the purées till just beginning to boil, and check the seasoning. Put at either end of a large, warmed dish – they should be just thick enough not to run into each other where they meet. Lift the chicken fillets with a perforated slice and pile in the middle. They should show white through the golden crumbs which adhere to them. Serve immediately.

5. Main Course Dishes: Vegetables with Cheese

Carrots, turnips and swedes are delicious peeled, finely sliced and boiled gently till just tender, put in an ovenproof dish, sprinkled thickly with grated cheese and browned in the oven. The six dishes given here are a little more unusual.

Brussels Sprouts Gratinées

For 4   1 lb (½ kg) Brussels sprouts
3 rashers of bacon, rather fat, cut in small pieces
2 oz (60 g) cheese, grated
1 oz (30 g) breadcrumbs
croûtons

The sprouts must be firm and hard, not leafy and not too large. Boil till just tender and drain well. Meanwhile fry the bacon, drain, and keep hot in a fireproof dish. Toss the sprouts in the bacon fat for 2 or 3 minutes, so that they are lightly fried all round – do not have the fat too hot when doing this. Lift them out with a slice or perforated spoon and add them to the chopped bacon, lightly mixing all together. Sprinkle thickly with cheese and crumbs, brown under a hot grill, and serve as a starting course or a supper dish, with croûtons of fried bread. Also very good served with cold meat.

Celeriac with Cheese and Walnuts

This is a most excellent dish to serve with a good burgundy or claret. With lamb chops it makes a good, substantial main course. Served with crisp toast and a green salad it is enough on its own for a lighter meal.

Celeriac is a large, irregularly shaped root, available in most greengrocers from Christmas to March, but not as much used in this country as it should be. It tastes strongly of celery and has a pleasant turnip-like consistency. The point of this dish is the combination of the celery, walnut and cheese flavours.

For 4
2 lb (1 kg) celeriac
2 lb (1 kg) carrots
1 lb (½ kg) turnips
8 oz (240 g) onions
salt and black pepper
1½ oz (45 g) butter
6 oz (180 g) shelled walnuts, coarsely chopped
4 oz (120 g) Cheddar cheese, grated

Peel the large root or roots of celeriac, cutting them for convenience of peeling. Cut the pieces into fairly even-sized chunks, about ½ × 1½ inches (1 × 3 cm). Drop the chunks into boiling salted water, boil for 10 minutes, and drain. (The celeriac requires separate boiling from the other vegetables in the first place, to get rid of any bitterness.)

Peel the carrots, turnips and onions in the usual manner, and cut into pieces about the same size as the celeriac. Boil together for 15 minutes, and drain. Butter a wide, shallow, ovenproof dish. Mix the celeriac with the other vegetables and season, using scant salt but plenty of pepper. Put them in the dish, spreading the top flat. Dot with butter and cover with foil. Cook in the oven at 350°F, gas mark 4, for 20 minutes. Remove from the oven, scatter with the walnuts and then with the cheese. Return to the oven and bake near the top for a further 15 minutes or until the cheese is melted and beginning to brown. The cheese protects the walnuts, which are apt to brown very quickly.

The dish can be prepared at any convenient time up to the point where it is finally baked.

Cucumber and Cheese Mousse

The most delicious of dishes for lunch on a hot summer's day, or for a starter for a dinner party on a warm evening. The mousse can be made the day before and kept in the refrigerator. If it is a main course for lunch, it is made in a ring mould, the centre being filled with the prawn or chicken mixture given below. If it is a starting dish it requires no additions, and may be made in individual soufflé dishes and turned out. Serve on a bed of crisp, pale lettuce leaves.

For 6   1 pint (6 dl) aspic jelly, made according to directions on packet
8 oz (240 g) Danish blue or Stilton cheese
juice of ½ lemon
white pepper
8 oz (240 g) double cream
8 oz (240 g) cucumber, peeled and finely diced
lettuce
12 thin slices of cucumber and a tablespoon of finely chopped parsley to garnish

Allow the jelly to cool and just begin to set. Break the cheese into small pieces and put into a liquidizer. Add the jelly, lemon juice and pepper. Liquidize until of the consistency of thin cream. The colour will be slightly grey. Pour into a bowl and stir in the cream, mixing well. Stir in the diced cucumber. Pour into a ring mould and put in the refrigerator for at least 2 hours or overnight.

Turn out on to a bed of lettuce. Arrange cucumber slices round the mould or put one or two on each individual mould, sprinkle with parsley and serve.

FILLINGS FOR CENTRE IF REQUIRED:
(*1*) 8 oz (240 g) frozen prawns, defrosted
2 hard-boiled eggs, finely chopped
4 oz (120 g) diced cucumber
salt and pepper

Mix lightly with a fork and pile into the middle of the mould.

(*2*) 8 oz (240 g) finely chopped chicken
2 oz (60 g) finely chopped walnuts
flesh of 1 avocado, cut in ¼ inch (½ cm) cubes
salt and black pepper

Mix lightly with a fork, season rather highly and put in the middle of the mould.

Leeks with Cheese Sauce

For 4   8 leeks
½ pint (3 dl) white sauce
2 oz (60 g) grated cheese
breadcrumbs
1 oz (30 g) butter

Wash the leeks very carefully, removing all grit and roots. Boil them gently until tender. When cooked, press well as they hold a good deal of water. Cut into small pieces. Mix the white sauce with the grated cheese. Butter a fireproof dish, put a layer of sauce in it, then a layer of chopped leek, and continue until all are used. Sprinkle the top with breadcrumbs and dot with butter. Stand the dish in a tin with a little cold water in it, and bake for about 10 minutes in a hot oven, about 450°F, gas mark 8.

September Supper

This is a dish for a late summer evening, when the first chill of autumn can just be felt but when gardens and shops are full of marrows and tomatoes, onions and corncobs. Frozen or tinned corncobs can be used in this dish, but fresh kernels have a different texture and more flavour. This supper dish is best accompanied by crusty bread or toast and butter.

For 6   3 oz (90 g) butter
2 large onions, peeled and finely cut in rings
1 young green marrow, peeled, halved lengthways, seeded and cut into 6 pieces
2 corncobs, husked
8 oz (240 g) mushrooms
1 lb (½ kg) tomatoes, blanched and quartered
salt and freshly ground black pepper
6 oz (180 g) Cheddar cheese, grated

First, heat 2 oz (60 g) of butter and gently fry the onions until light golden-brown. While they are cooking, poach the pieces of marrow gently in boiling salted water for 10 minutes. Have ready a large shallow dish, warmed and lightly buttered, and lay the cooked marrow in it so that the other vegetables can be piled on the separate slices. Boil the corncobs for 15 minutes, remove from the water, hold upright on a chopping board and, slicing downwards, strip off all the kernels. Put some on each marrow slice till all are used, and keep warm.

Lightly fry the sliced mushrooms and tomatoes together and season. Put the onion on the corn, and the mushrooms and tomatoes on top of it. Some of the vegetables will overflow between the slices of marrow. Cover each piled marrow slice with grated cheese, and bake the dish for 10 minutes in a hot oven (400°F, gas mark 6,) near the top, so that the cheese just browns. Lift the marrow slices out whole with a slice, and spoon some of the juice and extra vegetables on to each plate.

A Spinach Supper Dish

This is very quick and easy to make if you use frozen vegetables. Four individual ovenproof dishes are needed, each large enough to take a good helping of vegetables. Sausages are good served separately if you want a more substantial dish.

For 4   2 large packets frozen spinach, chopped or leaf
1 lb (480 g) frozen mixed vegetables, preferably including corn
2½ oz (75 g) butter
2 tablespoons thick cream
salt and freshly ground black pepper
4 oz (120 g) Cheddar cheese, finely grated
4 slices white or wholemeal bread, each cut into two triangles and lightly fried (these can be cooked earlier and reheated if more convenient)

Cook the spinach and mixed vegetables according to the directions. Drain well, and put the spinach through a blender or food mill. Stir in the butter, add the cream, and season to taste, while stirring over a low heat. Set aside. The purée should be a little thicker than double cream. Butter the individual dishes, and put a quarter of the mixed vegetables in each. Pour a quarter of the spinach purée over each, sprinkle each one with a quarter of the grated cheese, and bake in the oven at 400°F, gas mark 6, for about 8 minutes. The tops should be golden brown. When serving, stick a corner of two croûtons in each dish, so that they stand up like sails. Serve the dishes on plates and eat with teaspoons.

6. Main Course Dishes: Vegetables with Eggs

Vegetables and eggs are a natural marriage, particularly in omelettes and soufflés. Soufflés do not appear very early in English cookery, but the omelette, first known as a 'herbolace' and later often known as an 'amulet', goes back to the Middle Ages. All those given here make an excellent main course for lunch or supper and all are quick and easy to make.

Eggs Aggrandized

This makes a delicious and rather grand main course, if two eggs are served for each person. It is fairly light and could well be followed by an Apple Charlotte with cream. If it is to be served as a starting course, serve one egg per person and use half the quantities of pastry and vegetables.

For 4 8 oz (240 g) puff pastry (frozen is excellent)
8 oz (240 g) tomatoes
8 oz (240 g) mushrooms
1 oz (30 g) butter
8 eggs
salt and pepper
¼ pint (1½ dl) good béchamel sauce
2 tablespoons double cream
2 teaspoons finely chopped tarragon, fresh or dried
2 teaspoons finely chopped parsley

Prepare the pastry earlier in the day on which the dish is to be served. Roll it out about ¼ inch (½ cm) thick and leave to rest for 10 minutes. Cut into 4 equal pieces, each large enough to hold 2 eggs. Trim the edges. Place on a baking tray and bake at 450°F, gas mark 8, for 10 minutes or until golden brown. Set aside until needed.

Blanch the tomatoes and cut them in ¼ inch (½ cm) slices. Put these in a small buttered dish to warm through at the bottom of a moderate oven. Finely slice the mushrooms and sauté lightly in butter. Place with the tomatoes to keep warm and place the tray of pastry to heat through, just above them. Melt the butter and pour a little into a large, shallow, ovenproof dish. Break the eggs carefully on to it, sprinkle with salt and pepper, and pour over the remaining butter. Place the dish near the top of the oven. Heat the béchamel sauce and stir in the cream and tarragon. As soon as it reaches boiling point, set it aside to keep warm. Check the eggs. If the whites are just setting, it is time to assemble the dish while they finish cooking.

Put the hot pastries on a flat serving dish or on individual plates. Put some of the tomato slices on each and the mushrooms on the tomatoes. When the eggs are ready, cut round each egg white and lift the egg very carefully on to the mushrooms, two to each pastry slice. As soon as all eight are in place, pour over the sauce. Sprinkle lightly with parsley and serve.

OMELETTES

Most people have their own particular way of making omelettes, but when vegetable fillings are to be used the best results are sometimes obtained by cooking the mixture on one side and finishing under the grill instead of folding over. The following recipes are for slightly unusual vegetable fillings, except for the classic 'fines herbes'. It is best to make the omelettes when everyone is already seated at table. A six-egg omelette can be made in a fairly large pan and successfully lifted. An eight-egg omelette is better made as two or as four individual omelettes.

Asparagus Omelette (1)

For 4   32 green asparagus tips, cooked, well drained and
                seasoned and kept hot, *or* 1 large tin
             1 oz (30 g) butter
             6 eggs, beaten
             seasoning

If using tinned asparagus, warm gently in half the butter. Heat the rest of the butter in a heavy pan and pour in the seasoned eggs. Put the asparagus tips on one half as it begins to set, and fold the other half over. Slide on to a hot plate to serve.

Asparagus Omelette (2)

This is a very pretty dish, usually served individually as a starting course. It depends on quick, neat cooking and making up.

For 4 32 heads of green asparagus *or* 16 heads of very large blanched asparagus
8 eggs, well beaten and seasoned
salt and pepper
butter

Cut the asparagus heads so that there is about 1½ inches (3 cm) of stalk. Boil gently in salted water till just tender and drain well. Make four small round omelettes, working the mixture with a spatula to keep them in small circles about 3 inches (6 cm) in diameter. Spoon the hot butter over them. As soon as they begin to set, lift them on to four small, warmed plates and quickly stick the asparagus heads upright into each. Serve at once.

Omelette of Courgettes and Mushrooms

This should be made as two omelettes, or as four individual omelettes.

For 4 4 oz (120 g) mushrooms, finely chopped and lightly sautéed in butter
4 oz (120 g) courgettes, very thinly sliced, unpeeled, and sautéed till just beginning to brown
salt and freshly ground black pepper
8 eggs, well beaten and seasoned
2 oz (60 g) butter

Mix the mushrooms and courgettes and season rather highly. Keep hot in a medium oven or in a small pan over low heat. Pour half or a quarter of the egg mixture into very hot butter and when the omelette is cooked as you like it, put some of the vegetable mixture on one half, fold the other over it and serve immediately, either as a whole omelette or divided in two.

Omelette aux Fines Herbes

This is probably the most famous of all omelettes. Two recipes are given here, both excellent. Some people prefer one and some the other. The third recipe is for an omelette aux fines herbes plus, the plus being a very small quantity of a rather luxurious vegetable or shellfish.

For 4	8 eggs	
	seasoning	
	1 oz (30 g) butter	
	1 tablespoon parsley	all very
	1 teaspoon thyme	finely chopped
	12 or so chives	and mixed
	1 teaspoon marjoram (oregano)	together

(1)

Beat the eggs well, season, and pour half quickly into a pan in which half the butter has been made smoking hot. Cook fast, working round the edges with a spatula, for one minute. Spoon half the chopped herbs on to one side, fold the other half over and keep hot on a warmed dish while the second omelette is made.

(2)

Proceed as above, but mix the herbs into the beaten eggs before making the omelettes in the usual way. They will be fairly evenly distributed throughout the finished omelette.

(3)

Make exactly as No. 2 above, but just before folding over, place on one half one of the following:

> 4 oz (120 g) tuna fish
> 4 oz (120 g) crab (fresh or tinned)
> 4 oz (120 g) mushrooms
> 4–6 cooked artichoke bottoms
> 4 oz (120 g) prawns
> 4 oz (120 g) cooked peas or broad beans (preferably fresh)

All the above should be cut into small ¼–½ inch (½–1 cm) pieces, sautéed in very little butter, seasoned, mixed with a tablespoon of double cream and kept warm (not boiling) until the omelette is ready. Spoon in two separated heaps on the same half of the omelette and fold the other half over.

Mushroom or Tomato Omelette

For 4 1 oz (30 g) butter
8 eggs, well beaten and seasoned
4 oz (120 g) mushrooms, finely chopped and lightly sautéed, *or* 6 oz (180 g) tomatoes, skinned, quartered and fried in butter for 3 or 4 minutes

Heat the butter in a heavy pan, pour in half the beaten eggs and, as they begin to set, add half the mushrooms or tomatoes and fold the egg mixture over. Serve and repeat.

Pipérade

This dish from the Basque country makes a complete meal. The strong flavours of the combined vegetables give it a stimulating quality. It should be accompanied by fresh, crusty bread and rough red wine.

For 4 2 tablespoons cooking oil
2 large onions, skinned and roughly chopped
2 cloves garlic, skinned and finely chopped
3 large red or green peppers, stems, cores and pips discarded, and flesh cut in ½ inch (1 cm) strips
2 lb (1 kg) tomatoes, blanched and quartered
1 tablespoon mixed thyme and marjoram, fresh or dried
salt and black pepper
6 eggs, well beaten
1 tablespoon finely chopped parsley

Heat the oil in a large deep frying pan. Gently fry the onions and garlic until they are just tender but not browned. Stir in the strips of peppers and cook for a further 5 minutes, stirring frequently. Add the tomatoes, the thyme and the marjoram and mix well together. Season with salt and pepper. Allow to boil briskly, to reduce some of the juice. After 8–10 minutes, the vegetables should be ready. Stir in the beaten eggs, and continue to stir until all the egg appears creamy and slightly set. Check the seasoning. Sprinkle with parsley and serve immediately. Once the eggs are added the company should be seated and waiting for the dish.

Potato and Onion Omelette

An open, flat omelette, containing small crisp, fried croûtons of bread. Delicious for supper with young fresh vegetables.

For 4   1 oz (30 g) butter
1 tablespoon cooking oil
8 oz (240 g) onions, peeled and very finely sliced
8 oz (240 g) cooked potatoes, cut in ½ inch cubes
2 slices of bread, crusts removed, cut in ½ inch
   squares and fried crisp in a little butter
6 eggs
salt and pepper

Heat the butter and oil in a heavy frying pan and fry the onions gently until they are just beginning to colour. Drain and keep warm. Fry the potatoes in the same oil and butter, very gently, so that they are heated through but hardly coloured at all. Drain and mix with the onion. Add the prepared croûtons and keep warm.

Make the omelette as usual, seasoning well, and cook on one side until the top is just beginning to set. Pour on to it the potato mixture, and hold the pan under a pre-heated grill until the omelette is set and the eggs rising and beginning to brown among the vegetables. Serve direct from the pan on to hot plates, cutting the omelette across and across into quarters.

The Prior's Omelette

This is an inimitable omelette, worthy indeed of the greediest prior. The recipe comes from the town of Montfort, outside Paris. It requires only crusty bread, a rather sharp green salad and a bottle of red wine to make an outstanding meal. You will need a very hot grill to finish the omelette.

For 2   ½ pint (3 dl) good cheese sauce
2 oz (60 g) double cream
2 oz (60 g) finely grated Cheddar cheese
1 oz (30 g) grated Parmesan cheese
2 oz (60 g) walnuts, very finely chopped

6 eggs
salt and freshly ground black pepper
2 oz (60 g) butter
1 tablespoon parsley, very finely chopped

Make the cheese sauce, stir in the cream and keep hot over boiling water. Mix the grated cheese and the walnuts, put in a small saucepan, and stand over boiling water so that the cheese just begins to soften. Stir a little. Make the omelette, which should not set in the middle. As soon as it begins to do so, spoon the cheese and walnuts gently on to one half and sprinkle with half the parsley. Fold the omelette over, and carefully slide on to a large flat warm dish. Pour over the hot cheese sauce, and put the dish under the grill until it begins to bubble and brown (about 2 minutes.) Remove, sprinkle with the remaining parsley, and serve at once.

Spanish Omelette

This makes a substantial supper dish for four people. A large pan is needed and the grill must be pre-heated. Green beans or peas can be added if liked.

For 4
2 medium onions, finely sliced
3 oz (90 g) cooking oil
2 oz (60 g) butter
8 oz (240 g) cooked potatoes, cut in dice
4 medium tomatoes, skinned and cut in quarters
1 green pepper, seeds removed and cut in ½ inch
   (1 cm) pieces
4 pork sausages, cut in rings
4 rashers of bacon, cut in ½ inch (1 cm) pieces
1 clove garlic, crushed, *or* ½ teaspoon garlic salt, if
   liked
pepper and salt
8 eggs

First gently fry the onions in half the oil and 1 oz (30 g) of butter so that they become soft but only just beginning to brown. Set aside to keep warm in a large bowl and lightly fry the potatoes. Add these to the onions and keep both warm. Put the remaining oil in the pan and fry the tomatoes and green peppers together. Lift and add to the onions and potatoes. Fry the sausages and bacon together till just cooked but not too crisp. Add to the vegetables and mix all lightly together. Season with garlic, pepper and salt. Keep warm.

Beat the eggs well, season lightly, pour into the bowl of prepared ingredients and stir all together. Tip into the pan of hot butter and fry till the egg is just setting, working it away from the sides of the pan. When set, hold the pan under the pre-heated grill for a minute or two, until the top just begins to brown. Serve direct from the pan on to heated plates, cutting the omelette in four sections and lifting each out with a slice or spatula.

Spinach Omelette

This nineteenth-century recipe was intended to be made up as a large omelette for two people. It makes a complete supper dish, satisfying and delicious.

For 4   4 oz (120 g) frozen spinach, defrosted
1 tablespoon double cream
1 hard-boiled egg, finely chopped
salt and pepper
¼ teaspoon grated nutmeg
4 eggs
1½ oz (45 g) butter
1 large slice white bread, cut into ½ inch (1 cm)
    squares, fried crisp in half the butter on both sides
    and kept warm

Stir the very well-drained spinach into the cream and heat very gently till almost boiling. Stir in the chopped hard-boiled egg. Season with salt, pepper and nutmeg, and keep warm. Make the omelette in the usual way. Spoon the spinach mixture along one half and sprinkle the croûtons over it. Fold over the other half. Divide across the middle when serving.

SOUFFLÉS

Soufflés are very easy to make provided the whites and yolks of the eggs (always one or two more whites than yolks) are beaten very well and the flavouring sauce is ready and waiting at a lukewarm temperature, neither hot nor cold. A proper soufflé dish (or individual soufflé dishes) with straight sides is best because the mixture heats and rises evenly, but a deep ovenproof bowl can be used successfully. The oven should be pre-heated to 450°F, gas mark 8, and the door opened very quickly and gently once during the cooking time (approx. 20 minutes), to see if the soufflé is becoming too brown. If it is, a piece of foil can be laid lightly over the top.

When cooking a soufflé everything should be done very quickly from the moment when the eggs and the sauce are combined. A soufflé cannot wait for those who are to eat it once it has left the oven – everyone should be seated at the table waiting for it.

Tomato Soufflé

For 4   1 oz (30 g) butter
½ pint (3 dl) fresh tomato purée (see p. 31)
1 tablespoon tomato paste
¼ pint (1½ dl) béchamel sauce
salt and freshly ground black pepper
¼ teaspoon dried sweet basil, pounded to powder
5 egg yolks, well beaten
6 egg whites, beaten to hold a peak

Butter a soufflé dish well. In a saucepan, mix the tomato purée with the tomato paste and béchamel sauce and heat gently over a low heat. Season highly with salt, pepper and basil. When just luke-warm, add the well-beaten egg yolks and stir over low heat for 5 minutes. The mixture must on no account boil. Remove from the heat and fold in the egg whites, as fast as possible, but lifting from the bottom without violent stirring. When the mixture is fully amalgamated, turn it into the buttered dish and cook according to the directions above.

Mushroom Soufflé

For 4   1 oz (30 g) butter
¼ pint (1½ dl) béchamel sauce, made extra thick
½ pint (3 dl) mushroom purée (see p. 29)
salt and freshly ground black pepper
5 egg yolks, well-beaten
6 egg whites, beaten to hold a peak

Butter a soufflé dish well. Heat the béchamel sauce and mushroom purée gently together and season well. While still only warm, add the beaten egg yolks and stir over a very low heat for 5 minutes. Do not allow to boil.

Remove from the heat and fold in the egg whites. Turn into the soufflé dish and bake.

Asparagus Soufflé

The asparagus must be fresh. Frozen or tinned asparagus does not give a good flavour.

For 4   24 heads of large blanched asparagus, *or* 48 heads of
              thin green asparagus

Boil the trimmed and washed asparagus till just tender. Cut off the heads and reserve. Put the tender part of the stalks through a food mill and then strain into a saucepan. There will be an ounce or two of liquid. Stir ½ pint (3 dl) of béchamel sauce into this and season highly. Add the egg yolks in the usual way and stir the asparagus heads into the mixture just before adding the egg whites. Cook as for tomato soufflé (p 99).

7. Main Course Dishes: Vegetables in Pastry

Pies and pasties were very important to our ancestors from the Middle Ages till the end of the nineteenth century. A feast day pie of the sixteenth or seventeenth century was generally made of a 'coffin' of rich pastry, raised by hand and filled with meat or game, packed round with many tit-bits, filled up with gravy and, often, rosewater, vinegar and melted butter, and covered with a pastry lid, over which sugar was often scraped. For Lent and other fasts, fish pies were made, with salt cod or herrings taking the place of meat and the tit-bits consisting of artichoke bottoms, mushrooms, almonds, walnuts, slices of orange or lemon, truffles and hard-boiled eggs. A few recipes for 'herb' pie have come down to us, also intended for fasting. In most of these, the chopped vegetables are piled in the pastry coffin and the pie filled up with beaten eggs and milk, so that the vegetables are set in a custard. Open tarts were sometimes made, 'as large round as cartwheels', and the most usual fillings were a purée of spinach with currants or prunes, or a mixture of pounded chicken in a white sauce to which such delicacies as artichokes, mushrooms, cockscombs and 'raisins of the sun' were added.

In fact, vegetables and pastry are a particularly satisfactory combination. The pies, tarts, quiches and vol-au-vents which follow are all delicious, some filled with bacon, chicken or prawns combined with a vegetable and some with a vegetable filling only.

Vegetable Pie with Potato Pastry

This is a very old recipe, intended to be eaten in Lent when meat was forbidden by the Church. Hot and filling, it is generally much liked by children. Any variation on the suggested vegetables can, of course, be used.

FOR THE PASTRY

For 4

6 oz (180 g) butter or margarine
8 oz (240 g) self-raising flour
salt
8 oz (240 g) cold cooked mashed potato
a little milk to mix

Rub the butter into the flour until you have a breadcrumb consistency. Stir in 1 teaspoon of salt. Work the mixture into the potato and then mix in a little milk. Work all together and turn. A blender makes this quicker. Place on a floured surface and knead until the dough appears smooth and fairly soft. Roll out and line a large, shallow ovenproof dish. Bake blind at 400°F, gas mark 6, for 15 minutes or until light golden brown.

FOR THE FILLING

8 oz (240 g) frozen mixed vegetables, cooked and
     allowed to cool (or stir-fry vegetables or fresh
     vegetables, in all cases diced, cooked and allowed
     to cool)
4 oz (120 g) mushrooms, sliced, lightly sautéed and
     allowed to cool
1 large or 2 medium onions, peeled, finely sliced,
     lightly fried and allowed to cool
¼ pint (1½ dl) white sauce
salt and pepper
3 oz (90 g) grated Cheddar cheese
1 beaten egg yolk

Mix all the vegetables into the sauce and season to taste. As soon as the pastry is cooked and has cooled a little, put in the mixture, lightly spread it so that it is smooth and even and sprinkle with the cheese. Brush the pastry all round with the egg and return to the oven to heat the vegetables. This will take about 15 minutes. The cheese should be melted and just beginning to brown. If the pastry is becoming too dark, cut a rough frame from kitchen foil and lay it over the dish so that the pastry is covered and the centre left uncovered to brown.

QUICHES

A quiche differs from a savoury tart because the filling is always based on a custard of eggs and milk or cream. The most famous is Quiche Lorraine.

Basic Quiche Recipe

For 4–6   1 large packet frozen short pastry
4 eggs
2 oz (60 g) double cream
½ pint (3 dl) milk, or ¾ pint (4½ dl) if cream is
    omitted

Roll out the pastry about ⅛ inch (¼ cm) thick and line a 10 inch (20 cm) flan tin, being careful that there are no holes in the pastry. Lay a piece of foil on top and sprinkle with small weights or dried beans. Bake at 400°F, gas mark 6, for 15 minutes. Take out of the oven and remove the foil and the weights.

Put in the chosen filling, pour over the egg mixture, return to the oven and bake for a further 30 minutes.

Brussels Sprout and Bacon Quiche

For 4   12 oz (360 g) cooked Brussels sprouts, fresh or
    frozen, but they must be very small
4 rashers streaky bacon, cut into small pieces with
    scissors, and fried just crisp
freshly ground black pepper

Put the cooked Brussels sprouts in a single layer on the pastry, and sprinkle the bacon between them. Season rather highly with black pepper and pour over the egg mixture.

Brussels Sprout and Chestnut Quiche

As previously, but instead of bacon substitute 12 oz (360 g) chestnuts, peeled and boiled till just tender in ½ pint (3 dl) of boiling water to which a knob of butter has been added. It does not matter if some of the chestnuts are broken. Drain and mix lightly with the Brussels sprouts. Put into the pastry case and pour the egg mixture over.

Quiche Lorraine

For 4   8 oz (240 g) lean bacon, cut into small pieces and
lightly fried until just beginning to brown on both
sides

Sprinkle the bacon into the pastry case and pour the egg mixture over.

In France, lean belly of pork, cut into dice, boiled for 5 minutes and then drained and fried as above, is preferred to bacon. Some recipes include very finely chopped onion, fried till just tender and mixed with the bacon.

Mushroom and Bacon Quiche

For 4   8 oz (240 g) mushrooms, finely sliced
1½ oz (45 g) butter
3 rashers of bacon, cut into thin strips

Sauté the mushrooms in the butter. Lightly fry the bacon and mix with the mushrooms. Spoon the mixture all over the bottom of the cooked pastry case and pour the egg mixture over.

Onion Quiche

For 4   12 oz (360 g) onions, peeled and finely sliced
3 oz (90 g) butter

Sauté the onions gently in the butter until they are soft but not coloured. Spread over the bottom of the cooked pastry case and pour the egg mixture over. Top with grated cheese if liked.

Tomato and Green Pepper Quiche

For 4   1 lb (½ kg) tomatoes
1 large green pepper
2 oz (60 g) butter for frying
1 oz (30 g) Cheddar cheese, grated

Blanch, quarter and lightly fry the tomatoes. De-seed the pepper, chop into 1/4 inch (½ cm) pieces, and fry in the same pan until soft. Mix the tomato and the pepper together, spread over the pastry case, and pour the egg mixture over. Sprinkle the grated cheese over the top, if liked.

OPEN SAVOURY TARTS

Open savoury tarts are well suited for serving at summer lunches or suppers. Eight different fillings are suggested here. Serve with a sharp green salad and crusty bread and butter.

To make the pastry base, line an 8–10 inch (16–20 cm) flan tin with shortcrust pastry, frozen or home-made, being careful not to make any hole or gap between bottom and sides. Cover the bottom with foil, and weight with dried beans or peas or the special small metal weights now on sale for this purpose. Bake at 400°F, gas mark 6, for 15 minutes. Remove the weights and foil and bake for another 5 minutes. Allow to cool slightly.

Tart of Artichokes with Chicken Fillets

This is a grand and delicious savoury tart and should be made in a shell of puff or flaky pastry in a 10 inch (20 cm) flan tin. It is best of all with an orange, watercress and hearts of lettuce salad, with a good French dressing, and with a bottle of chilled, dry white wine.

Line the flan tin with puff or flaky pastry which has been rolled out very thin, left at least 10 minutes to rest, and rolled again. Weight it with foil scattered with beans or baking weights. Bake in an oven pre-heated to 450°F, gas mark 8, for 15 minutes. Remove, lift off the foil and weights and, with a sharp, pointed knife, cut round and lift off the centre (which will have risen slightly in spite of the foil and weights). Brush over the sides with beaten egg, and return to the oven for 5 minutes to crisp the centre. Allow to cool.

For 6–8   4 oz (120 g) flour
          salt and black pepper
          1 teaspoon finely chopped fresh tarragon (dried can
            be used if fresh is not available)
          12 artichoke bottoms (tinned will do, as fresh are
            very expensive)
          3 oz (90 g) butter
          6 breast portions of chicken, defrosted if necessary,
            roasted and allowed to cool
          ¼ pint (1½ dl) double cream
          1 tablespoon very finely chopped parsley

Mix the flour with ½ teaspoon salt, ¼ teaspoon black pepper and the tarragon. Drain the artichoke bottoms well and allow to dry a little. Dip them in the seasoned flour and fry in the butter for 3 minutes on each side. They should not brown, but the flour should be just golden. Lift out and keep warm.

Remove the white meat from the chicken joints. There should be two fairly large pieces for each. (The remaining darker meat can be chopped and used for sandwiches, or as part of a casserole, and the bones for stock.) Cut each piece of white meat lengthways in two. Dip in the seasoned flour and fry very lightly in the pan used for the artichokes, turning them on all sides. Again, they should not brown, but just begin to colour.

Lay the artichoke bottoms like a pavement all over the bottom of the pastry shell, cutting a few in halves if necessary to make them fit. Pour a little of the cream over them and then lay the twenty-four chicken fillets to cover the artichokes. Pour the remaining cream over them and lightly place a piece of foil over the top. Put into a pre-heated oven at 350°F, gas mark 4, for 15 minutes. Take out, remove the foil, and sprinkle all over with the parsley. Serve at once.

Cheese and Leek Tart

For 4   8 oz (240 g) leeks, well washed and cut in 1 inch
             (2 cm) lengths
         1 oz (30 g) butter or margarine
         1 oz (30 g) flour
         4 oz (120 g) Cheddar cheese, finely grated
         1 egg, well beaten
         a little milk
         salt and freshly ground black pepper

Put the leeks into boiling, salted water to cover, and gently boil till soft. Drain well, reserving the liquid, and allow to cool. Make a roux of the butter and flour, stir in the liquid from the leeks, and when smooth, add the cheese. Stir until the cheese has melted and combined with the sauce, and then add the egg. If very thick, stir in a little milk. Season to taste. Spread the leeks over the bottom of the pastry shell, pour the cheese and egg mixture over them and put in an oven pre-heated to 400°F, gas mark 6, for 10 minutes. The cheese filling should be puffed up and golden brown. Serve immediately.

Tart of Ham and Tomato

A fine dish for August when tomatoes are plentiful and well-flavoured from garden or shop. Very good with a green salad or with a dish of spinach.

For 4–6   1 lb (½ kg) tomatoes, blanched and skinned
1 teaspoon sweet basil (fresh or dried)
2 teaspoons caster sugar
salt and freshly ground black pepper
4 gammon rashers, fried so that they are just
  beginning to brown
1 small onion, skinned and very finely chopped
½ oz (15 g) butter

Halve the tomatoes crossways and lay them neatly all over the bottom of the tart case. Sprinkle with the basil and half the sugar, and season with a little salt and plenty of pepper. Cut the gammon rashers into strips about 1½ inches (3 cm) long and ½ inch (1 cm) wide. Lay them all over the tomatoes. Sprinkle over the remaining sugar and the finely chopped onion. Dot with the butter in very small pieces. Bake in a pre-heated oven at 350°F, gas mark 4, for 15 minutes, checking after 10 minutes that the onion is not darkening too much. If it is, lightly cover with foil. Remove from the oven and serve immediately. The onion should be slightly crisp.

Tart of Mixed Vegetables

For a quick dish, use frozen vegetables. If you have a kitchen garden, use your own peas, carrots, small onions or shallots, and small French beans. Both are good, but naturally the garden vegetables have more flavour and the textures are more varied.

For 4   ½ pint (3 dl) white sauce, into which a little cream
  has been stirred
8 oz (240 g) frozen mixed vegetables, defrosted *or*
  about 8 oz (240 g) garden vegetables, pre-cooked
salt and pepper
1 tablespoon grated Parmesan cheese

Heat the sauce, stirring all the time, and as it comes to the boil, add the vegetables. Stir them in, check the seasoning, and at once fill the pastry shell. Sprinkle with the cheese and put into the oven pre-heated to 400°F, gas mark 6, for 10 minutes. Serve immediately.

Mushroom Tart with Walnuts

For 4   1 lb (½ kg) mushrooms
2 oz (60 g) butter
juice of ½ lemon
salt and pepper
2 tablespoons double cream
4 oz (120 g) walnuts, coarsely chopped
1 tablespoon finely chopped parsley

Cut the stalks level with the caps of the mushrooms. Sauté the whole caps in the butter very gently till just tender, turning them once. Lift them with a perforated slice on to a piece of kitchen roll and leave so that any surplus butter is absorbed. Chop the stalks finely and fry for 2 minutes in the pan in which the mushrooms cooked. Spoon them over the bottom of the tart and arrange the mushroom tops over them, gills upwards, fitting them closely. If there are too many for a single layer, arrange the spare ones in a partial second layer. Sprinkle with lemon juice, salt and pepper. Spoon the cream over them so that a little goes into each cup. Put in an oven pre-heated to 350°F, gas mark 4. Fry the walnuts in the mushroom pan, very gently as they catch easily, stirring and turning them. After the tart has been in the oven for 15 minutes, take it out and sprinkle the walnuts over it. Put back for another 5 minutes and serve immediately, sprinkled with parsley.

Onion Tarts from St Rémy

St Rémy is a small town in Provence. These little tarts are a local speciality, and some years ago were served to us at a country restaurant and a few days later at the house of friends in the area. They are served very hot on a small plate for each person as an hors d'oeuvre. A central dish of vegetables such as sticks of celery, cucumber, raw carrots, green peppers, with small gherkins and olives, was placed on the table at the same time, on both occasions. Very good followed by roast lamb cooked with rosemary.

For 4   8 oz (240 g) shortcrust pastry
2 medium onions, peeled and chopped fine

1½ oz (45 g) butter
½ tablespoon plain flour
2 tablespoons milk
2 tablespoons double cream
a very little crushed garlic or ½ teaspoon garlic salt
salt and pepper
2 oz (60 g) finely grated Parmesan cheese

Line 12 very small bun tins with shortcrust pastry rolled very thin.
Set aside. Fry the onions very gently in 1 oz (30 g) of the butter in
a small, heavy pan, till tender but not browned. Stir in the flour,
cook for ½ minute without browning, and then stir in the milk.
When thick and smooth, stir in the cream. Remove from the heat
and stir in the garlic or garlic salt, and a little salt and white pepper.
Spoon into each pastry case but do not fill them quite full. Sprinkle
each with Parmesan cheese and put a tiny dab of the remaining
butter on each. Put in the pre-heated oven, near the top, at 400°F,
gas mark 6, for 10 minutes. Remove and serve immediately. The
tarts should be very small, very neat (no filling bubbling over) and
very hot. Many people eat three.

Tarte Provençale

All the flavours of a hot summer in the south of France are combined
in this dish, which is really better made for a party of six or eight
than for four. For a fine country summer lunch, serve with red
wine, crusty bread and butter and three or four small, very brown
sausages for each person. The quantities given are for a 10 inch
(20 cm) flan tin.

For 4   1 green pepper, seeded, chopped into ¼ inch (½ cm)
                pieces and lightly fried
            8 oz (240 g) tomatoes, blanched and quartered
            1 large onion, skinned, finely sliced and lightly fried
                until just soft
            2 oz (60 g) mushrooms, sliced and lightly fried
            ½ teaspoon dried rosemary
            salt and pepper
            2 tablespoons white sauce into which 1 tablespoon of
                double cream has been stirred
            2 oz (60 g) walnuts, coarsely chopped

In a bowl, lightly mix the green pepper, tomatoes, onion and mushrooms. Add the dried rosemary and season lightly with salt and pepper. Spread the white sauce and cream mixture over the pastry, and then pour in the vegetable mixture. Level it with the back of a spoon, and bake for 10 minutes in an oven pre-heated to 350°F, gas mark 4. Take it out and sprinkle the walnuts all over. Return to the oven for 5 minutes and serve immediately.

Spinach and Egg Tart

For 4   1 oz (30 g) butter ·
1 large packet frozen chopped spinach, defrosted and
    drained
salt and freshly ground black pepper
2 tablespoons double cream
4 hard-boiled eggs

Melt the butter in a heavy saucepan. Put in the spinach and stir until beginning to boil. Add salt and pepper to taste. Remove from the heat and stir in the cream, mixing well. Allow to cool a little, then fill the pastry shell. Cut all the eggs in quarters lengthways and arrange on the spinach so that they form the petals of a flower. Press these petals gently into the spinach so that they are just embedded. Return to the oven for 5 minutes and serve very hot.

Vol-au-vents

Frozen vol-au-vent cases ready for baking are so good and easily obtainable that it is hardly worth the considerable trouble of making puff pastry and preparing them at home. The frozen cases can usually be bought in two sizes, and two (or even three) of the larger size make a good main course, while the small ones are easy to eat in the fingers at parties. Many different fillings are suitable, but they should all have the main ingredients chopped very small, in ¼ inch (½ cm) cubes, bound together by a rather thick, well-flavoured sauce. A few suggestions for fillings are given below.

For a main course, two well-cooked vegetables such as peas, carrots, broad beans, French beans or spinach set off the appearance and the flavour of all these vol-au-vents very well.

Chicken and Mushroom Vol-au-vents

For 4   8 larger size vol-au-vent cases
½ pint (3 dl) rather thick white sauce
2 tablespoons double cream
6 oz (180 g) cold, cooked chicken, mostly white meat
2 oz (60 g) mushrooms, finely chopped and lightly
  fried
¼ teaspoon dried tarragon (if liked)
salt and pepper

Bake the vol-au-vent cases and cut out the centres according to the
directions. This can be done several hours before they are needed if
more convenient. Allow to cool. Make up the white sauce and when
it has cooled for 10 minutes, stir in the cream. Chop the chicken
into ¼–½ inch (½–1 cm) pieces, mix with the mushrooms and the
tarragon, and stir into the sauce. Check the seasoning. Spoon into
the centre hollows of the vol-au-vent cases, filling them right to the
tops, but not overflowing. Stick the centre piece of pastry on the
top of each. Place on a baking tray and put into the centre of the
oven, pre-heated to 350°F, gas mark 4, for 10 minutes. If the pastry
begins to darken, lay a piece of foil lightly over the tray. Serve at
once.

Artichoke Vol-au-vents

For 4   12 small vol-au-vent cases
1 tin of artichoke bottoms
1½ oz (45 g) butter
a little lemon juice
salt and freshly ground black pepper
¼ pint (1½ dl) white sauce
2 tablespoons double cream
1 tablespoon finely chopped parsley

Prepare the vol-au-vent cases as in the previous recipe.
   Drain the artichokes well, cut them into ½ inch (1 cm) cubes,
and lightly fry them in the butter, turning so that they are just
beginning to colour on all sides. Put them on a piece of kitchen
paper to drain. Squeeze lemon juice over and sprinkle with a pinch
of salt and black pepper. Heat the white sauce, and when it is just
at boiling point stir in the cream and the parsley. Add the artichoke

cubes, folding them in gently, and fill and bake the vol-au-vents as in the previous recipe.

Celeriac Vol-au-vents with Almonds

Celeriac is in most greengrocer shops in the winter months. It tastes exactly like celery but has a smooth, firm consistency when cooked. This is a particularly delicious filling.

For 4   12 small vol-au-vent cases
1 root of celeriac, about 1 lb (½ kg)
squeeze of lemon juice
¼ pint (1½ dl) good white sauce, rather thick
1½ oz (45 g) blanched almonds, chopped fine
2 tablespoons double cream
salt and pepper

Prepare the vol-au-vent cases as before, p. 113.

Peel the root of celeriac, wash it well, and then cut into neat ½ inch (1 cm) pieces. Put into boiling salted water and cook till just tender (about 15 minutes). Drain well and squeeze the lemon juice over. Bring the white sauce almost to the boil, and stir in the celeriac, then the almonds and finally the cream. Mix gently together. Check the seasoning. Fill the vol-au-vents and put into the oven for 5 minutes to get very hot.

Crab Vol-au-vents with Cheese and Olives

A little cheese brings out the flavour of crab but too much hides it. These proportions are exactly right.

For 6   18 small vol-au-vent cases
¼ pint (1½ dl) very thick white sauce
2 oz (60 g) grated Cheddar cheese
1 large dressed crab *or* 2 small tins of crab
2 oz (60 g) green olives, preferably stuffed with
    pimento, each cut in half
2 tablespoons double cream
salt and pepper

Prepare the vol-au-vent cases as before, p. 113.

Bring the white sauce just to the boil and add the grated cheese, stirring until it is completely melted. Stir in the crab, the olives and the cream. Check the seasoning, fill the vol-au-vent cases, and heat through in the oven for 5 minutes.

Mushroom Vol-au-vents

For 6   18 small vol-au-vent cases
2 oz (60 g) butter
8 oz (240 g) mushrooms, finely chopped
2 teaspoons lemon juice
1½ oz (45 g) plain flour
½ pint (1½ dl) milk
2 tablespoons double cream
salt and freshly ground black pepper

Prepare the vol-au-vent cases as before, p. 113.

Melt the butter in a heavy saucepan without allowing it to colour at all. Tip the mushrooms into it and fry gently for 2 minutes. Stir in the lemon juice, then the flour, and cook for a further 2 minutes. Stir in the milk and continue stirring till the sauce is smooth and thick. Add the cream and stir well. Check the seasoning, fill the vol-au-vent cases, and heat through in the oven for 5 minutes.

8. Main Course Dishes: Vegetables with Rice

Rice was first brought into England in about 1390, and up to the seventeenth century was regarded as an exotic and fairly expensive luxury. It was available in some of the great London markets and was bought in small quantities by the wealthy. The head gardeners of more than one great house tried to grow it in shallow troughs in hot houses, but with little success. Nowadays, rice is relatively cheap and many different varieties are packaged and easily available. The kind preferred for different dishes is in general a matter of personal taste, though certain guidelines apply. A pilaff or a paella is very good made with a large-grain Italian rice. For a successful pudding or a cold creamed rice, it is essential to use a short-grained, soft rice, such as Carolina. Brown rice is excellent in all savoury rice dishes, but looks less attractive than white. Its advantages are that it contains vitamins which are refined out of white rice. In a diet where rice is the staple food it is, therefore, much better, but in a good mixed diet it is not important to use brown if white is preferred. Wild rice, not always easy to obtain, is delicious cooked with an equal quantity of a long-grain white rice. It has a special, subtle flavour and the husks make the texture of the dish more interesting.

Paella

Paella is one of the most famous dishes in Spanish cooking, and is well worth making for its subtle flavours and the clear golden colour of the saffron-cooked rice, served steaming hot with joints of lightly browned chicken and delicious pink prawns.

Chicken (or sometimes duck or game birds) is always left in joints in a paella and served one joint to each person on a mound of rice and vegetables. Prawns are also generally part of the dish, and the combination of their delicate flavour with the chicken or game is outstanding. The prawns used vary from the freshwater crayfish or large Mediterranean prawns, to the smaller species to which we are more accustomed. Traditionally they are left in the shell in a paella but, outside Spain, many people prefer them shelled.

A paella is a very good dish for a supper party, so a recipe for eight is given. It requires only crusty bread and butter and a green salad as accompaniments.

For 8   4 tablespoons olive oil
8 chicken joints, not too large
8 oz (240 g) tomatoes, blanched, skinned and
    quartered
1 teaspoon paprika
2 pints (1 litre) chicken stock (can be made with a
    cube)
1 teaspoon powdered saffron
8 oz (240 g) French or any green beans, topped and
    tailed and cut into 1 inch (2 cm) lengths
8 oz (240 g) frozen peas, defrosted
12 oz (360 g) frozen shelled prawns, defrosted
4 oz (120 g) mushrooms, finely sliced and sautéed
2 cloves of garlic, peeled and crushed
4 oz (120 g) almonds, coarsely chopped and fried
    light brown in 1 oz (30 g) butter
salt and pepper

Make the olive oil hot in a large skillet or frying pan about 2–3 inches (4–6 cm) deep, and fry the chicken to a crisp golden brown on all sides (about 15 minutes). Lift it out on to a plate. Put the tomatoes into the oil, add the paprika, and fry for 3 minutes, turning. Add the chicken stock and bring to the boil. Add the chicken joints, saffron, beans and peas and cook for 7 minutes. Now add the rice, prawns, mushrooms, garlic, almonds, 1½ teaspoons of salt and ½ teaspoon of pepper. Stir gently, lifting the chicken joints to the top each time. In 20–25 minutes, the rice should be perfectly cooked and all the stock absorbed. If by any chance it requires a little further cooking, pour in ¼ pint (1½ dl) of boiling water, stir gently but thoroughly and allow to boil until the rice is exactly as you like it.

PILAFFS

A good pilaff is attractive to look at, interesting to eat, and provides a good well-balanced meal in itself. The rice for a pilaff should always be cooked in stock. Traditionally, it is cooked covered in the oven and allowed to stand, still covered, for a few minutes to allow the flavours of the various ingredients to permeate the rice while the cooking of the meat is completed.

A great variety of ingredients may be used, and the cost and luxury of the dish naturally varies with them. One of the great hotels of Venice, the Gritti Palace, used to serve lobster pilaff as one of its chief specialities. To sit on the terrace above the blue water, hungry from a morning of wandering and intensive looking, and be elegantly served with this entirely delicious and highly decorative dish, was a perfection of sensuous pleasure. It was also outrageously expensive.

A pilaff made with green peas, fresh thyme and parsley and a little mint, chopped hard-boiled eggs and some tiny squares of very crisp fried bread, served in an English garden to a hungry family and friends on a rare warm summer evening, is as decorative as the lobster, as elegant if piled in a handsome dish, as delicious and satisfying and extremely cheap.

For a main supper dish, a vegetable pilaff, with or without eggs, can have chopped cooked chicken or pork, small squares of gammon, small sausages cut in rings, or prawns cut in halves added when the rice comes out of the oven. These ingredients should be heated for 10 minutes wrapped in buttered foil, while the rice is still cooking on the heat.

Grated cheese, in particular Parmesan, is often, though not invariably, served with a pilaff.

The rice for a pilaff must be the long-grained Patna type, which can be used alone or mixed with wild or brown rice. Wild rice is expensive and not always easily available. Brown rice can be obtained at most health-food shops and good supermarkets. It can be used without white rice, if preferred.

The rice for a pilaff should be cooked as follows:

For 6   1 oz (30 g) butter *or* 1 tablespoon cooking oil
             8 oz (240 g) rice
             1 pint (6 dl) stock (can be made with a stock cube)

Melt the butter or heat the oil in a wide, heavy or non-stick pan
with a lid. Stir in the dry rice. Add the stock, stirring well, and then
the other ingredients which you are using. Bring to simmering point
over gentle heat, and continue to simmer until all the liquid is
absorbed. Do not stir while it is cooking. After 40–45 minutes,
check that all the liquid is absorbed, cover again, and stand off the
heat on the side of the stove, or in a warm place, for 5–10 minutes,
so that the steam inside the pan can finish the rice and blend in the
flavour of the final ingredients.

A Fine Chicken Pilaff

This is a complete meal in itself. It is good made in small quantities
or for a party, and needs no accompaniment but a green salad.

For 6–8   1 large onion, very finely chopped
cooking oil and 1 oz (30 g) butter
4 oz (120 g) mushrooms, finely sliced
½ teaspoon garlic salt or 1 crushed clove of garlic
8 oz (240 g) long-grain white rice
4 oz (120 g) brown or wild rice
8 oz (240 g) shelled peas, fresh or frozen
1 teaspoon turmeric
1 teaspoon cumin
¼ teaspoon mace and ¼ teaspoon powdered ginger
salt and freshly ground black pepper
1 pint (6 dl) chicken stock (made from the bones and
carcass of the chicken, or from a stock cube if time
is short)
all the meat from a cooked chicken, without skin or
bone
4 oz (120 g) blanched almonds, cut in quarters
lengthways
2 oz (60 g) seedless raisins, soaked for a few minutes
in hot water and drained

Cook the onion gently in the bottom of a large casserole, using
cooking oil. When it is tender but not brown, add the mushrooms
and cook for a further 3 minutes, stirring. Add the garlic and stir in
all the rice, the peas, the spices and 1 teaspoon of salt, unless the
stock is highly seasoned. Mix well, pour in the stock, bring to the

boil, cover, and put into the oven pre-heated to 350°F, gas mark 4, for 30 minutes.

Meanwhile chop the chicken into ½ inch (1 cm) pieces and lightly fry in butter. Set aside and fry the almonds in the same pan, stirring all the time till a light golden brown. Take the pilaff from the oven and stir in the chicken and the raisins, making sure that all is well mixed. Check the seasoning, adding a little black pepper, and return to the oven for a further 10 minutes. Remove, lightly stir in the almonds, cover and allow to stand for 10 minutes in the warming drawer or any warm place. Turn on to a warmed, shallow dish to serve, so that the pilaff is piled up.

Lobster Pilaff

Quite a small lobster, less than 1 lb (½ kg) in weight, will make a luxurious dish for six people, expensive but delicious. The rice is cooked by a different method and the pilaff should be served in individual dishes. This dish must taste as fresh as the sea, but rich from the cream and delicately seasoned with the spices. Serve with plenty of fresh, dry, hot toast.

For 6   8 oz (240 g) white Patna rice
¼ pint (1½ dl) double cream
1 small lobster, shelled, coral and clawmeat reserved, flesh chopped, and antennae kept for decoration (wrap clawmeat in a piece of buttered foil and heat in oven for last 10 minutes before dishing rice)
4 oz (120 g) shelled prawns, fresh or frozen, each cut in half
4 oz (120 g) button mushrooms, finely sliced and lightly sautéed in butter
1 teaspoon finely chopped fresh tarragon
½ teaspoon mace
½ teaspoon turmeric
sea salt and freshly ground black pepper
1 tablespoon sherry

Bring the rice to the boil in 2 pints (1 litre) of salted water, and boil rapidly for 20 minutes. Check to see if the grains are soft and swollen. If not, cook for another 5 minutes. When ready, drain immediately through a sieve or colander and run the cold tap through the rice, lifting and stirring. Drain again, shaking well. Every grain should be separate, firm and yet tender. Set aside. Heat the cream in a large saucepan till almost boiling and stir in the chopped lobster, the prawns and the mushrooms. Simmer for 3 minutes, stirring gently. Then stir in half the rice, add the tarragon, mace, turmeric and black pepper, then add the remaining rice, still stirring. Stir very gently over a low heat for a minute only, add the sherry and the lobster coral, stir again, and spoon into six individual dishes. Garnish each with the hot clawmeat and a long whisker, and serve immediately.

Oriental Pilaff

This pilaff can be curried or highly seasoned as preferred. It is always made with lamb or chicken and may include all or only some of the ingredients listed. It is very good for a supper party, served with a green salad and crusty bread and butter.

For 6–8
1 medium onion
1 clove of garlic, skinned and finely chopped
3 oz (90 g) cooking oil
10 oz (300 g) long-grain rice
1 pint (6 dl) any good stock
8 oz (240 g) cooked lamb or chicken (without skin or gristle), chopped into ½ inch (1 cm) pieces
4 oz (120 g) mushrooms, sliced
4 oz (120 g) raisins, pre-soaked in warm water for a few minutes and drained
2 oz (60 g) stoned and halved black olives
1 teaspoon ground coriander
½ teaspoon ground turmeric
½ teaspoon dried rosemary
2 teaspoons good curry powder, if this is to be used
2 oz (60 g) fresh or canned pineapple, cut into ½ inch (1 cm) pieces
4 oz (120 g) almonds, skinned and finely chopped
salt and freshly ground black pepper

Lightly fry the onion and garlic in the oil till just tender. Add the rice, all the stock, the meat, mushrooms, raisins and olives, and all the spices (including the curry powder if using). When the rice is ready to remove from the heat, add the pineapple and the almonds, and season well. Cover and allow to stand in a warm place for 10 minutes. Serve piled on a flat dish, accompanied by soy sauce and mango chutney if liked.

Pilaff of Peas with Eggs

For 6   1 onion, peeled and chopped very fine
3 oz (90 g) butter or 3 tablespoons cooking oil
8 oz (240 g) rice (Patna, Basra or brown, or a mixture)
8 oz (240 g) shelled peas, fresh or frozen and defrosted
1 teaspoon finely chopped thyme (fresh if possible)
1 pint (6 dl) chicken stock (can be made with a stock cube)
4 eggs
1 teaspoon finely chopped mint (fresh if possible)
1 tablespoon finely chopped fresh parsley
2 large slices white bread, crusts removed, cut in very small squares
salt and pepper

Fry the onion gently in half the butter or oil until soft and transparent. Stir in the rice, the peas and the thyme. Add the stock, stir, and cook gently until all the liquid is absorbed. Meanwhile, hard-boil and finely chop the eggs, mix together the chopped mint and parsley, and fry the squares of bread very crisp in the remaining butter or oil. When the rice is cooked, remove from the oven and stir in the eggs and herbs. Season. Allow to stand, covered, in a warm place for 10 minutes. Stir in the crisp fried bread just before serving, mixing it in very lightly. Serve piled on a flat dish.

Sea Food Pilaff with Broad Beans

This is unusual and delicious. The flavour of the broad beans enhances that of the haddock and the prawns.

For 4   8 oz (240 g) shelled broad beans, fresh or frozen
1½ oz (45 g) butter
1 tablespoon cooking oil
1 teaspoon salt

½ teaspoon black pepper
½ teaspoon ground mace
½ teaspoon turmeric
4 oz (120 g) long-grain rice
¾ pint (4½ dl) chicken stock
2 fillets fresh haddock, defrosted if frozen
¼ pint (1½ dl) milk
4 oz (120 g) frozen prawns, defrosted and cut in
    halves
1 tablespoon finely chopped parsley

Cook the broad beans in boiling salted water for 15–20 minutes until tender. Drain and keep warm, adding ½ oz (15 g) of butter.

Heat the oil and the remaining butter together in a heavy saucepan. Stir in the salt, pepper, mace and turmeric and add the rice. Stir until it is lightly coated with oil and well mixed with the spices, then stir in the stock and simmer till all the liquid is absorbed.

Meanwhile poach the haddock fillets gently in the milk for 5 minutes. Lift them out, remove all the skin and divide them into firm flakes. Keep warm. Reheat the milk till almost boiling and drop the prawns into it; bring just to the boil again and drain. Add them to the flaked haddock and stir both into the rice as soon as all the stock is absorbed. Add the broad beans last, mixing them in very lightly.

Cover and put in a warming drawer or very low oven for 5 minutes. Check the seasoning and serve piled on a flat dish, sprinkled with parsley.

Chicken and Vegetable Risotto

For a true risotto, the rice is lightly fried in olive oil with onions and garlic before adding the stock, in which it finally cooks. This gives a different texture from a pilaff. A large-grained rice is needed for perfection. The grains of Patna rice are too small and dry.

For 4–6   2 pints (1 litre) chicken stock (may be made from
        cubes)
    3 tablespoons olive oil
    1 large onion, peeled and very finely sliced
    2 cloves garlic, peeled and crushed

8 oz (240 g) large-grained rice

8 oz (240 g) tomatoes, blanched, skinned and roughly chopped

1 teaspoon finely chopped thyme, fresh or dried

pinch of rosemary, fresh or dried

4 oz (120 g) mushrooms, sliced and sautéed in butter

4 oz (120 g) cooked chicken, all skin removed and cut into ½ inch (1 cm) pieces

2 oz (60 g) shelled walnuts, roughly chopped

2 oz (60 g) sultanas, soaked in warm water for a few minutes

1 green pepper, de-seeded, chopped into ¼ inch (½ cm) pieces and lightly fried

salt and black pepper

Keep the chicken stock just on the boil on a very low heat. Heat the oil in a large open pan or skillet, and put in the onion and the garlic. Fry gently until the onion begins to soften but not to colour. Stir in the rice and turn it in the oil several times. Then stir into it about a quarter of the stock, and add the tomatoes and herbs. Stir again and simmer till the rice has absorbed all the liquid. Immediately, stir in about three-quarters of the remaining liquid and gently mix in the mushrooms, chicken, walnuts, sultanas and green pepper. Stir until almost all the stock is absorbed and check the rice, which may be exactly as you like it, but will probably need the small remaining quantity of stock stirred in and a further few minutes cooking to absorb it. Season with salt and freshly ground black pepper when checking the rice, and serve very hot.

9. Main Course Dishes: Fruit and Vegetable Recipes Using Breadcrumbs, Toast or Slices of Bread

This section is a small collection of outstanding dishes, most of them very simple, in which bread is a main ingredient. Most of them are traditionally English dishes which occur in very early cookery books and manuscripts. A few are French and Italian.

They are very suitable for the present decade because bread is expensive and the last few slices of a loaf are apt to be wasted; they make an interesting change from the potato, pasta or rice which are so often used to fill out made dishes of meat, cheese and vegetables; most of the savoury dishes are fairly light and convenient to eat, either while watching television or at a party.

SPREAD TOASTS

In the Middle Ages, the long trestle tables which were set up for the main meal in the great halls of noble houses and manors were laid out with large slices of coarse bread, known as 'trenchers' (from the French *tranche* – a slice) and used as plates. Sometimes the trencher was wholly or partially eaten and sometimes it was not. At the lowest tables the trenchers were very often devoured by hungry outdoor servants, who got no more than cheese and sometimes a piece of better quality bread to put on them. At the high table, gold or silver plate was expected, and for the middle ranks, wooden or pewter plates replaced the trenchers. Strangely, however, the edible plate early developed into a fashion for 'toasts', and there are various recipes for spread toasts and 'enriched toasts' in medieval and Elizabethan times. In medieval times, good white bread was toasted on a gridiron, soaked in spiced wine, and then re-crisped and served with almond, milk or curds. A dish called 'Toast Royal' was served at great feasts. Wine, nuts, 'raisins of the sun', sugar and nutmeg were mixed and boiled with rice flour to thicken the mixture, which was spread hot on trenchers of toasted Manchet bread (the finest), decorated with shapes cut from sugar-plate and gilded. 'And lay, for a lord, in a dish, fair trenchers and serve it forth.' By the time the dish reached the lord, it would certainly have been cold. No one dining in state ever ate hot food before the nineteenth century. Another 'spread toast' was called Pokerounce, the spread being hot spiced honey, thickened with a 'panada' (breadcrumbs soaked in milk). Elizabethan spread toasts were often savoury. Veal and chicken, eggs and cheese were used in various ways. Salt fish and fish roes were spread on toast for Lent or other fast days.

The toast for these dishes should always be freshly made and hot. In some instances it should be lightly spread with butter or margarine, but many of the fillings should be spread direct on the hot, dry toast. One slice from a large loaf, white or brown as preferred, is allowed for each person in the following recipes.

Celery and Ham Toast

For 4   12 sticks good celery, carefully washed and trimmed,
                with some of the strings removed
             2 oz (60 g) butter
             1 oz (30 g) flour
             3 tablespoons milk
             salt and pepper (less salt if celery salt is used)
             pinch celery salt if available
             4 slices hot toast, buttered
             4 slices gammon, lightly fried, cut in ½ inch (1 cm)
                pieces and kept warm
             1 tablespoon finely chopped parsley

Cut the prepared celery into ½ inch (1 cm) pieces and cook them in boiling salted water until tender (about 20 minutes). Meanwhile, melt the butter, stir in the flour to make a roux, cook for 1 minute and stir in the milk. Stir until it boils, season with pepper and salt and celery salt, and boil for 2 minutes. The resulting sauce should be very thick. Set aside. Drain the celery (reserving the water) and mix into the sauce. This will thin the sauce slightly and the resulting mixture should be just thick enough to stay on the toast. If too thick, stir in a very little of the reserved water in which the celery cooked. Make the toast and lay the gammon pieces on it. Spoon the hot celery mixture on to the gammon, sprinkle with chopped parsley and serve immediately.

A very good alternative is to sprinkle the celery mixture with grated cheese and brown the toasts under the grill.

Creamed Smoked Haddock and Tomatoes on Toast

These spread toasts were appreciated during the long Lenten fasts, when no meat was allowed except by special dispensation to the sick. A version is mentioned in the household books of the Earl of Northumberland in the sixteenth century.

For 4   6 smoked haddock fillets (frozen)
¼ pint (1½ dl) milk
4 tomatoes
1½ oz (45 g) butter
1 oz (30 g) flour
1 tablespoon double cream
black pepper
4 slices hot buttered toast
1 tablespoon finely chopped parsley

Skin the haddock fillets while still frozen and poach them in the milk, adding 2 tablespoons of water. Blanch and chop the tomatoes roughly, fry lightly in a little butter and keep warm. As soon as the fish is cooked (about 10 minutes) lift the fillets from the liquid and flake them carefully, removing any remaining skin and any stray bones. Set aside.

Melt 1 oz (30 g) butter and stir in the flour to form a roux. Stir in the cooking liquor, add the cream and then the flaked fish. Season with black pepper only. Keep warm while you make the toast. Spoon some chopped tomato on to each slice, pile the haddock mixture on top, sprinkle with parsley and serve.

Green Beans and Walnuts on Toast

This is very simple and delicious. It makes an unusual starting course, or a light main dish after a substantial soup. Whole French beans must be used.

For 4   1 lb (½ kg) young French beans
4 slices hot toast, buttered
1 oz (30 g) butter
salt and freshly ground black pepper

2 oz (60 g) finely chopped walnuts
1 tablespoon finely chopped parsley

Cut the ends off the beans and lay them, all lying parallel, in a wide, shallow pan of boiling, salted water. The water should just cover them. Simmer till just tender (about 10 minutes). Meanwhile, make the toast and lightly butter each slice. Lift the beans with a pierced slice, draining well, and lay them lengthways on each toast. Sprinkle first with pepper, then thickly with the walnuts. Top with the parsley and serve immediately.

Onions and Green Peppers on Toast

For 4   2 oz (60 g) butter or oil
4 medium onions, peeled and finely sliced
2 green peppers, halved and seeded and coarsely
    chopped
4 slices hot dry toast
salt and freshly ground black pepper

Heat the butter or oil and fry the onions and peppers together till soft and beginning to brown and crisp. Just before they are ready, make the toast. Lightly season the vegetables and spoon them on to it. Serve very hot.

Poached Egg and Spinach on Toast

Traditional, and very quick to make if you use frozen chopped or puréed spinach.

For 4   2 large packets frozen chopped or puréed spinach
salt and pepper
1 oz (30 g) butter
1 oz (30 g) flour
2 tablespoons cream
1 oz (30 g) grated Cheddar cheese
4 eggs
4 slices hot buttered toast

Cook the spinach with a little salt and no additional water until melted and just boiling. Drain and set aside. Make a roux with the butter and flour and stir the spinach directly into it. Stir till it comes to the boil and then stir in the cream. Taste and season, sprinkle with the cheese, and keep warm while you poach the eggs. Place one egg on each toast and serve at once.

FILLED AND BAKED BREADS

Filled breads were served in noble households in the Middle Ages. Meat and certain vegetables which, since the eighteenth century, have always been seasoned with salt, were quite frequently sweetened with honey or sugar and dried fruits, and flavoured with rose water or orange flower water. The sweet, enriched and stuffed breads would have been eaten with the roast meats and birds, much as we eat pastry or potatoes. 'Wastels yfarcel' were small loaves of fine, white bread from which all the crumb was scooped and mixed with finely chopped suet, currants, 'raisins of the sun' and various spices. The stuffing was then pressed back into the loaf, which was damped with milk and re-baked for a short time and served hot.

In the fifteenth century, 'Rastons' became popular. An enriched dough was used, and when the small loaves had been baked, their tops were cut off, in the manner of a crown. The crumb was then taken out and made into coarse crumbs which were mixed with a large quantity of butter and put back into the shell. The top was put on and the Raston replaced for a short time in the oven and served 'all hot'. Such breads were only for those at the high table.

The popularity of filled breads declined as that of pastry increased, but they were still popular for grand picnics and sometimes for shooting lunches in the nineteenth century. In the recipes which follow, the crisp bread makes pastry or potatoes superfluous. The dishes are unusual today but, once served, will be asked for again.

Mushrooms and Ham in Crisped Rolls

Best of all with an orange and watercress salad.

For 4   4 crisp round rolls
                3 oz (90 g) butter
                2 gammon steaks (¼ lb (120 g) each)
                12 oz (360 g) mushrooms, finely sliced
                black pepper

Cut the tops thinly from the rolls, and scoop out the crumb. Rub them over with butter. Do not butter the insides. Bake at 300°F, gas mark 2, for 10 minutes or until crisp. Keep warm. Cut the trimmed gammon steaks into strips about ¼ inch (½ cm) wide and then cut across twice so that none are larger than 1 inch (2 cm). Fry them gently in 1 oz (30 g) of butter till they are glazed and tender. Lift and keep warm. Fry the mushrooms in the same pan, using the remaining butter. They should be tender in 3–4 minutes. Mix the gammon into them, season lightly with black pepper and spoon the mixture into the rolls. Serve on a hot dish immediately.

Prawns or Chicken with Herbs in Crisped Rolls

The tarragon with either the chicken or the prawns enhances their flavour.

For 4 4 crisp round rolls
1 oz (30 g) butter
8 oz (240 g) cooked chicken, all skin and bone
removed and cut into ½ inch (1 cm) pieces, *or* 8 oz
(240 g) frozen prawns, defrosted and drained
1 teaspoon finely chopped tarragon
1 teaspoon finely chopped parsley
½ pint (3 dl) béchamel sauce, made rather thick
salt and pepper

Prepare the rolls as in the previous recipe. Stir the chicken or prawns and the tarragon and parsley into the hot béchamel sauce, bring to simmering point, stirring all the time, and simmer for one minute. Check the seasoning and keep warm until the rolls are ready. Fill and serve immediately.

Omelette Fines Herbes in French Bread

The appearance of a long loaf or rolls as a supper dish is surprising and the delicious omelettes inside very pleasing. Serve with a dressed mixed salad.

For 4 1 long French loaf (not a stick) *or* 4 long, crusty rolls
2 oz (60 g) butter
6 eggs
salt and pepper
2 teaspoons mixed parsley, thyme and marjoram,
finely chopped *or* 2 tablespoons finely grated cheese

Cut one end from the loaf or one from each roll. Scoop out as much crumb as possible, taking care not to break or pierce the crust. Using a long knife, butter the inside of the loaf or rolls and then rub the outside over with butter. Rub the cut-off end with butter. Place all on a baking tray and bake in an oven pre-heated to 300°F, gas mark 2, for 20 minutes, by which time the bread should be very crisp and golden outside and fairly crisp within. Put to keep warm, low down in the oven.

While the bread is crisping, beat and season the eggs for the omelette, and as soon as the bread is put to keep warm, make the omelette as usual using a pan of about the diameter of the length of your loaf. (A soufflé omelette is not suitable.) Sprinkle in the herbs or cheese while the centre of the omelette is still not set and then fold it over twice with a spatula so that it is narrow enough to slip into the bread. Hold the end of the bread close to the pan, lift the omelette on the spatula and slip it in. Put the loaf on a warm dish. Prop the crust against the cut end and serve at once, cutting into four portions at table.

If rolls are used, it is best to make four tiny omelettes, two at a time, in the pan.

Green Butter Bread

Serve very hot on a separate hot plate, with any grilled meat or fish and fresh or frozen green peas. Alternatively, serve with cold ham and a good mixed salad.

For 4   4 oz (120 g) butter, softened

1 tablespoon parsley
2 teaspoons thyme
1 teaspoon marjoram   mixed and very
1 leaf sage   finely
2 teaspoons chives   chopped

1 small Coburg loaf or any round loaf with a crisp crust, new or one day old

Cream the butter and mix in the herbs. Cut the whole top from the loaf and reserve. Scoop out all the crumb from the loaf and the top and make into coarse crumbs in a blender or processor. Mix these into the herb butter, stirring well, and put the mixture back into the loaf. Replace the top. Stand the loaf in a baking tray and put in the oven pre-heated to 350°F, gas mark 4, for 15 minutes. By this time, the bread should be hot and some of the butter absorbed into the inside of the crust.

Hot Herb or Garlic Bread

Delicious with grilled chops, steaks or chicken, or with a cheese or tomato dish.

For 6–8   1 long loaf, large or small as required, white or brown as preferred, sliced ¼ inch (½ cm) slices (or use sliced bread)

4 oz (120 g) butter, softened

2 cloves of garlic, crushed, *or* 1 tablespoon finely chopped parsley and 1 tablespoon mixed thyme, rosemary, marjoram and chives, finely chopped

Work either the garlic or the parsley and mixed herbs into the butter. Spread each slice of bread with the mixture, putting them all together in the original shape of the loaf. Wrap loosely in foil and put in the oven pre-heated to 350°F, gas mark 4, for 30 minutes. Open the top of the foil after 20 minutes so that the crust can crisp. Serve very hot.

Tomato Charlotte

If you grow your own tomatoes, this is a dish to make when your crop is at the height of its yield. Small tomatoes can be used up this way. Served with a green salad or with French beans or peas, it makes a complete main course for lunch or supper.

For 4   2 lb (1 kg) tomatoes, blanched, skinned and halved or quartered

12 thin slices of white bread, from a large tin loaf

3 oz (90 g) butter

pepper, salt and caster sugar

1 teaspoon fresh or dried basil, if possible

2 oz (60 g) Cheddar cheese, grated

Butter all but 2 of the bread slices on one side, leaving the crusts on, and cut each slice into three. Butter the remaining 2 slices on both sides. Line a 2 pint (1¼ l) pie dish or other shallow, ovenproof casserole with bread, butter side down and outwards. Put in a layer of tomatoes, and season with a little salt, plenty of freshly ground black pepper and a sprinkling of sugar and basil, both of which bring out the flavour of the tomatoes. Cover this layer of tomatoes with the 2 slices buttered on both sides. Put in the remaining tomatoes, season, and cover with the remaining bread strips, buttered side downwards. Sprinkle the cheese over the top. Put into the middle of the oven pre-heated to 350°F, gas mark 4, and bake for 30 minutes. The cheese should be melted and browning but not dried up, and the bread should be crisp round the sides and at the bottom. Serve very hot.

10. Stuffed Vegetables

A plain baked tomato is pleasant, but a stuffed baked tomato is a treat. Aubergines, sweet peppers and vegetable marrows are all excellent when stuffed. Stuffed cabbage was considered fit for the highest tables, not only of England but of France and Russia also.

Stuffed tomatoes and peppers, in particular, are very good for a party supper as they can be made well ahead and are easy to serve and to eat. The stuffing can be elaborated by the addition of prawns, chicken or chopped mushrooms, and a vegetable purée and a green salad may be offered with them.

Recipes for traditional stuffings are given (see p. 34), and variations on them suggested for different vegetables to be served on different occasions. In all cases, the forcemeat can be prepared ahead and kept in the refrigerator until needed. Recipes for cold stuffed vegetables which make a good starting course are also given.

Stuffed Aubergines

Aubergines have a very subtle flavour and texture, and are best stuffed with chicken, pork or veal, though lamb is often used. A very grand and delicious party dish can be made by stuffing them with crab. The pulp, removed, diced and lightly sautéed, should always become part of the filling. Two recipes are given here.

Aubergines Stuffed with Crab

This is an early nineteenth-century recipe, originally from North Italy. Three aubergines and two crabs are required. The filled shells are served on a bed of rice into which peas have been mixed, or on a bed of spinach made into a rather stiff purée (see p. 31). The two filled crab shells are placed in the middle and the six aubergine half-shells all round. Each filled aubergine shell should be cut in half with a sharp knife and the halves arranged without separating them. Thus, each guest is served with a quarter shell and some extra filling from the crab shells.

For 10–12   3 aubergines
12 oz (360 g) fine white breadcrumbs
salt and freshly ground black pepper
1 oz (30 g) grated Parmesan cheese
4 oz (120 g) finely grated Cheddar cheese
1 teaspoon finely chopped tarragon
2 teaspoons finely chopped parsley
¼ teaspoon powdered mace
¼ teaspoon powdered ginger
2 dressed crabs in the shell
4 oz (120 g) butter
¼ pint (1½ dl) double cream

Cut the aubergines in half lengthways and remove all the pulp with a sharp knife, being careful not to pierce the skins. Lightly salt the inside of the skins and the pulp, stirring the salt in a little, and leave to stand for half an hour. Then rinse in cold water and drain. This removes the slight bitterness which is sometimes found in aubergines.

Meanwhile, prepare the breadcrumbs. Season about a quarter of them, and mix with the Parmesan cheese. Reserve these. Mix the Cheddar cheese, herbs and spices into the larger unseasoned quantity. Remove the meat from the crab claws, reserving all the claws for decoration. Chop the clawmeat roughly and reserve. Mix all the remainder of the crabmeat into the larger quantity of breadcrumbs. Chop the aubergine pulp into ½ inch (1 cm) cubes and sauté lightly in 2 oz (60 g) butter until they are soft and partly transparent (about 4 minutes). Stir the crab and crumb mixture into the hot pan with the aubergine pulp, and mix well, stirring in the cream to moisten a little. Fill the aubergine shells and the two crab shells and place all of them on a shallow fireproof dish or a baking tray.

Bake in the middle of the oven pre-heated to 350°F, gas mark 4, for 15 minutes. Remove and sprinkle each with the chopped claw meat. Cover with the reserved breadcrumbs and Parmesan mixture and return to the oven, this time near the top, for a further 20 minutes. Serve decorated with the crab claws, stuck into the ends of each shell.

Aubergines Stuffed with Lamb

This is a much simpler recipe than the previous one. Any cooked meat can be used, but lamb is traditional.

Prepare and cook 2 aubergines exactly as in the previous recipe, but fill with a mixture of the following:

For 4
8 oz (240 g) fine white breadcrumbs
8 oz (240 g) minced cooked meat
1 large onion, finely chopped and sautéed until soft
1 well beaten egg
3 oz (90 g) butter
¼ teaspoon sage
¼ teaspoon thyme
1 tablespoon finely chopped fresh parsley

Stuffed Cabbage

A very ornamental dish, best served with rice into which a few peas and some corn have been mixed. Small, whole tomatoes, blanched, baked and set round the cabbage, add to the appearance and the flavour of the dish.

For 4–6
8 oz (240 g) minced cooked ham or lamb
1 medium onion, finely chopped and fried until just softened
8 oz (240 g) fine white breadcrumbs
1 tablespoon parsley, finely chopped
1 teaspoon thyme, finely chopped
2 oz (60 g) finely chopped mushrooms, lightly sautéed
2 egg yolks, well beaten
1 green cabbage, pointed in shape and weighing 3 lb (1½ kg)
3 oz (90 g) butter
1 pint (6 dl) very good stock
1½ oz (45 g) flour

　　　　　salt and pepper (if ham is being used, salt very
　　　　　　lightly)
　　　　　a little lemon juice

Combine the meat, onion, breadcrumbs, herbs and mushrooms, and mix them well together. Stir in the beaten egg to bind.

Cut the stalk and any hard outer leaves from the cabbage. Put into boiling, salted water and cook for 10 minutes, then lift out and drain well. Place on a board and gently open out all the leaves, leaving the tender, pointed centre. Leave the cabbage to cool for 5 minutes. Starting from the centre, pile and spread a little stuffing upwards, first on the centre and then on each leaf, re-shaping the cabbage as you go. Tie the re-formed cabbage in three places with string. Melt half the butter in a large saucepan and stand the cabbage in it. Pour over it the well seasoned stock. Cover and simmer for 45 minutes, adding a little more stock if the first lot is much reduced.

After 45 minutes, test the cabbage with a skewer to make sure it is quite tender. Lift it on to a warmed serving dish and keep hot while you make a roux with the remaining butter and the flour and stir the stock into it, seasoning it lightly and adding a little lemon juice. Pour this around but not over the cabbage. Cut the strings and remove.

To serve, first place some rice on each plate, then cut the cabbage like a cake, lift each section out with a slice or spatula, and finally pour over 2 tablespoons of the sauce.

Stuffed Winter Carrots with Spinach Purée

This is a very pretty and unusual dish. Minced chicken instead of ham or lamb is very good in the stuffing.

For 4–6　　3 lb (1½ kg) large carrots
　　　　　　1½ pints (9 dl) stock
　　　　　　¼ pint (1½ dl) spinach purée (see p. 31)
　　　　　　12 oz (360 g) cooked long-grain rice
　　　　　　2 oz (60 g) melted butter
　　　　　　1 tablespoon orange zest

　　　　　　FOR THE STUFFING:
　　　　　　4 oz (120 g) minced cooked ham or lamb
　　　　　　1 small onion, finely chopped and fried until just soft

4 oz (120 g) fine white breadcrumbs
1 teaspoon parsley, finely chopped
½ teaspoon thyme, finely chopped
1 egg yolk, well beaten

Scrape the carrots and cut in halves lengthways. Cut out the centre cores with a sharp-pointed knife and discard or use in soup. Place the carrot halves in a shallow ovenproof dish or on a baking tray, and fill up with stock just to cover the carrots. Cook uncovered in the oven pre-heated to 350°F, gas mark 4, for 1½ hours.

Meanwhile, mix the stuffing ingredients and stir in the egg yolk to bind; prepare the purée and in the last half hour cook the rice. Take the carrots out of the oven and turn up to 400°F, gas mark 6. Pour off the stock and reserve to use for soup. Stuff each carrot half with the prepared mixture, piling it fairly high, put them back in the dish, and pour melted butter over each. Replace in the oven, near the top, to brown the stuffing a little.

Make sure the rice is hot and pile it in a rounded mound on a warm dish. Lean the carrots all round the mound of rice and serve the spinach purée separately in a sauceboat. Just before serving, sprinkle a pinch of orange zest on each carrot.

Stuffed Cucumber

These two extremely elegant recipes, one hot and one cold, were traditional in the eighteenth and nineteenth century but are almost forgotten today. Ridge cucumbers from the garden are as good as hot- or cold-house cucumbers, if they are young and firm. If they are home grown, taste a small piece to make sure there is no trace of bitterness.

Hot Stuffed Cucumbers

For 4   2 medium cucumbers
2 oz (60 g) butter
½ pint (3 dl) good, well-seasoned stock
1 tablespoon flour
1 tablespoon finely chopped parsley
1 tablespoon capers or small gherkins, cut in slices

FOR THE STUFFING:

4 oz (120 g) white cabbage, sliced very fine, cooked
   until just tender, and drained
1 small onion, chopped fine and cooked in ½ oz
   (15 g) butter until soft but not coloured
2 hard-boiled eggs, finely chopped
1 tablespoon parsley, chopped very fine
1 pinch grated nutmeg
salt and pepper

Peel the cucumbers thinly, cut off the stalk ends and remove all the centres, using a long, thin knife, such as a ham knife. Mix all the ingredients for the stuffing well together and spoon them into the hollow centres. Replace the stalk ends and fix with wooden cocktail sticks.

Melt the butter in a large, shallow fireproof dish or pan and very gently fry the cucumbers on all sides until very lightly browned. Pour off all the surplus butter (which can be used again) and pour in the stock. Simmer very gently for 15 minutes. Lift the cucumbers carefully on to a warm flat dish and keep hot.

Reheat a little of the butter in which the cucumbers were fried, stir in the flour, add the stock and stir until thickened. Check the seasoning carefully and pour over the cucumbers. Sprinkle the whole dish with parsley and capers or gherkins. This is very good served with hot, home-cooked gammon, roast pork or duck.

Cold Stuffed Cucumbers

A perfect summer light luncheon dish, served with brown bread and butter. The grapes can be replaced with cold cooked peas but, though good, the dish will have less distinction.

For 4

1 large cucumber
12 oz (360 g) green grapes
8 oz (240 g) cottage cheese
2 oz (60 g) double cream
salt and white pepper
2 hard-boiled eggs, finely chopped
1 tablespoon finely chopped parsley
1 crisp lettuce
French dressing

Peel the cucumber thinly and cut off the stalk end. Cut evenly in half lengthways and remove all the seeded centre from each half. Skin the grapes by dipping the bunches in boiling water for one minute, and remove the pips. Beat the cottage cheese with very little salt, the cream, and plenty of pepper. Stir in the chopped hard-boiled eggs. Fill half into the cavity of each cucumber half, and cover thickly with the grapes, leaving a few for the top. Lay on the remainder of the egg mixture, so that there is an even ridge along the cucumbers. Top with remaining grapes and sprinkle with parsley. Chill for a few minutes. Arrange the lettuce leaves on a flat dish and put the cucumbers on them. To serve, cut the cucumbers in halves crossways and serve with some of the lettuce, offering French dressing separately.

Dolmadis (Stuffed Vine Leaves)

The famous Greek dish of stuffed vine leaves can be made from the young leaves of an outdoor or coldhouse grape vine at any time from May to August. Choose the youngest and, therefore, lightest green leaves which are large enough to roll up. If necessary, two small leaves can be used, one on top and one underneath the filling, and tied in place. They can be served cold as a starter or hot in sauce as a main dish. As they are rather fiddly to make, it is worth making a double quantity and freezing half. If served hot, crusty bread and a tomato salad on a separate plate are the traditional accompaniments. Allow 3 dolmadis for each person.

For 4   12 vine leaves (or more if small)
1 pint (6 dl) good brown or chicken stock
¼ pint (1½ dl) dry white wine
½ oz (15 g) butter
½ oz (15 g) flour

FOR THE STUFFING:
6 oz (180 g) finely minced lamb
8 oz (240 g) cooked long grain rice
1 small onion, skinned and very finely chopped
1 oz (30 g) sultanas, soaked in warm water for a few minutes and drained
1 egg, well beaten
1 tablespoon finely chopped thyme, rosemary and parsley (dried will do)

¼ teaspoon each of powdered mace and turmeric
salt and freshly ground black pepper

Mix all the ingredients for the stuffing, adding the egg a little at a time and stirring well. Check the seasoning and form the mixture into 12 small rolls, each about 2½ inches (5 cm) long.

Dip each vine leaf, as you are about to roll it, into boiling salted water for a second, spread it flat, lay a roll of filling on it and roll and fold so that the filling is completely enclosed. Use two leaves if necessary. Tie each roll with thread, fine string or double cotton in two or three places, and lay them closely in a wide, shallow, fireproof dish. Pour the well seasoned stock over, bring to the boil, and simmer very gently for 30 minutes. Meanwhile, reduce the wine to about 2 tablespoons by fast boiling. Lift the dolmadis on to a flat serving dish and keep warm. Thicken the stock with a roux of the butter and flour, boil for 2 minutes, stir in the reduced wine and check the seasoning. Pour it round the dolmadis and serve.

If they are to be eaten cold, lift them from the stock with a perforated slice when they are cooked, allow them to cool and then chill for a few minutes. Serve with a slice of lemon for each person.

Stuffed Marrow Rings

For 4
    1 vegetable marrow, young and not too large
    1 oz (30 g) butter
    1 lb (½ kg) forcemeat for general use (see p. 35) *or*
       prune stuffing (see p. 34)
    4 oz (120 g) grated Parmesan cheese
    8 triangular croûtons fried bread

Peel the marrow and cut into 8 rings, each about 1 inch (2 cm) thick. Scoop out all the seeds from each ring. Simmer the rings very gently in boiling, salted water until tender (about 15 minutes). Carefully lift with a perforated slice on to a generously buttered fireproof dish or into shallow, individual dishes. Have ready and hot either the forcemeat or the prune stuffing (the prunes are very good with the marrow). Pile about 2 oz (60 g) into the centre of each marrow slice. Sprinkle with the cheese and brown under the grill. They may be kept hot for a few minutes in a warm oven. Serve with the croûtons.

Mock Goose

This is a cottage recipe going back to the eighteenth century, and probably earlier. The long shape of the finished dish looks rather like a roast goose, when nicely browned; there is no suggestion that it tastes like one, but it is very good in its own right. There are two versions – the first strictly vegetarian, the second with a proportion of sausage meat or finely chopped or minced ham. The vegetable marrow should be young and firm and about 12 inches (25 cm) in length.

Version 1
For 6
    3 oz (90 g) butter
    1 large onion, peeled and very finely chopped
    1 vegetable marrow, peeled
    8 oz (240 g) fine white breadcrumbs
    1 tablespoon finely chopped parsley (fresh or dried)
    1 teaspoon thyme, fresh or dried
    salt and freshly ground black pepper
    a little flour
    a pinch garlic salt

Melt 1 oz (30 g) of butter over a low heat and fry the onion until soft but not coloured. Meanwhile, cut a slice from the wider end of the marrow and set aside. Scoop out all the centre pips and pith with a long handled spoon or a spatula, taking care not to break through the skin of the marrow. When the onion is soft, mix the breadcrumbs and herbs and stir into the pan. Turn and stir for a minute or two until well amalgamated. Taste and season with salt and pepper. Spoon into the cavity of the marrow, pressing well in. Any surplus can be made into small balls and roasted round the marrow for the last 10 minutes of its cooking.

Put the lid on the marrow and, holding it upright, rub it lightly all over with flour and garlic salt. Put the remaining butter in a baking tray and lay the stuffed marrow on it, pressing the cut end well against one end of the tray. Bake for 35–40 minutes at 350°F, gas mark 4, basting several times. It should be tender and light golden brown in colour. Transfer to a warm serving dish, taking care not to break it. To serve, cut across in slices. It is good with rice and green beans or peas, and with tomato sauce or a good brown gravy.

Version 2

As above, but mix 6 oz (180 g) sausage meat or 6 oz (180 g) minced or finely chopped home-cooked gammon into the softened onion with the breadcrumbs and herbs. In this version, there will almost certainly be some stuffing left over to make forcemeat balls.

Chilled Stuffed Mushrooms

Very good as a summer hors d'oeuvre, served with crisp lettuce and thin brown bread and butter, or as an interesting garnish to a dish of cold meats.

For 4　　4 medium-sized mushrooms per person
　　　　　2 oz (60 g) butter to sauté mushrooms

　　　　　FOR THE GREEN BUTTER:
　　　　　4 oz (120 g) slightly salted butter, softened to room
　　　　　　temperature
　　　　　2 tablespoons finely chopped parsley
　　　　　1 tablespoon mint, chives, marjoram and thyme,
　　　　　　finely chopped together

Work the herbs into the 4 oz (120 g) of butter with a wooden spoon, or put all through a blender. The butter should appear a smooth light green, flecked all through with darker green.

Very lightly sauté the mushrooms in the 2 oz (60 g) of butter. Drain, cool and chill slightly. Spread the gill sides with the green butter and chill again.

Hot Stuffed Mushrooms

This is a delicious light supper dish. Two crisp bacon rolls for each person are excellent with the mushrooms, if liked.

For 4　　8 oz (240 g) forcemeat (see p. 35)
　　　　　16 large flat mushrooms
　　　　　4 oz (120 g) butter
　　　　　4 slices fresh, hot buttered toast, crusts removed
　　　　　2 oz (60 g) chopped walnuts

Warm the forcemeat through over a low heat and keep warm. Cut the mushroom stalks down to the level of the caps and chop them finely. Sauté the mushroom caps gently in half the butter, turning them over once. While they are cooking (about 6 minutes) make the toast, spread with the remaining butter and keep hot. When the mushrooms are done, put two on each slice of toast, gills upwards. Place a spoonful of forcemeat on each and fork it into a mound. Keep warm on a large flat dish. Fry the chopped mushroom stalks for 1 minute in the pan in which the caps were cooked. Stir the walnuts into them and fry for another ½ minute, stirring. Spoon over the stuffed mushrooms and serve immediately.

Stuffed Onions

For a splendid supper, serve with boiled rice and green peas or Brussels sprouts.

For 4
4 very large onions
4 oz (120 g) minced cooked meat, or chicken
8 oz (240 g) forcemeat (see p. 35)
a little flour, sugar, salt and freshly ground black pepper
3 oz (90 g) butter
½ pint (3 dl) good brown gravy to which a little sherry has been added

Peel the onions, cut off the tops and bottoms, leaving them whole, and parboil for 15 minutes in just enough boiling, salted water to cover them. Drain them well and scoop out the centres with a sharp, pointed knife, leaving walls about ½ inch (1 cm) thick. Finely chop the onion which has been removed and mix it with the minced meat and the forcemeat. Fill the onions carefully, and sprinkle with a little flour mixed with salt and pepper and a pinch of sugar. Butter a baking tray or fireproof dish and stand the onions in it. Melt the rest of the butter and pour over each onion.

Bake in the oven pre-heated to 350°F, gas mark 4, for 45 minutes, basting once or twice. The tops and outsides should be a rich golden brown. Serve the gravy separately.

Stuffed Green or Red Peppers with Tomato Purée

This is an old Provençal recipe, very good for lunch or supper in hot weather. It should be eaten with plenty of crusty bread.

For 4   4 large green or red peppers
2 medium onions, finely chopped
2 oz (60 g) butter
8 oz (240 g) cooked rice
6 oz (180 g) cooked minced lamb
1 tablespoon parsley, finely chopped
½ teaspoon thyme, finely chopped
½ teaspoon powdered turmeric
salt and pepper
2 oz (60 g) cooking oil

Plunge the peppers into boiling, salted water, boil briskly for about 3 minutes, and drain. Cut off the stalk ends, leaving a hole about 1 inch (2 cm) in diameter. With a pointed knife, remove all the seeds, being careful not to pierce the skins.

Fry the chopped onion lightly in the butter, using a large pan, and as soon as it is soft, stir in the rice and meat, mixing well together. Add the herbs, turmeric, salt and pepper and stir and turn for 2 minutes. Remove from the heat and carefully fill each pepper with the mixture, using a teaspoon. Pour the cooking oil into an ovenproof dish or a baking tray and lay the peppers in it. Spoon a little oil over each. Put into the middle of the oven, pre-heated to 400°F, gas mark 6, and cook for 20 minutes.

Serve very hot, with a purée of tomatoes (see p. 31) served separately.

Stuffed Baked Potatoes

Here are three very different ways of stuffing baked potatoes. A green salad is very good with all of them.

For 4   4 large (but not enormous) potatoes of fairly equal
size and even shape (the pink potatoes, generally
available, bake very well)
a little butter or cooking oil

Scrub the potatoes, removing all eyes, and just before baking make two holes in each with a skewer to prevent them bursting in the oven. (If the holes are made hours before baking, they may show up blackened when the potatoes are cut.) Rub the potatoes lightly all over with a very little butter or cooking oil. Place them on a baking tray and put in the oven pre-heated to 350°F, gas mark 4, for 1½ hours.

Version 1

> 1 oz (30 g) butter
> salt and freshly ground black pepper
> 4 eggs

Cut a lid lengthways from each baked potato and discard. Remove about a tablespoon of the inside from the lower halves, and lightly break up the remainder a little with a fork. Sprinkle well with salt and pepper, and put ¼ oz (7½ g) of butter in each central hollow. Break an egg carefully into each, and put back in the oven for 5 minutes or until the eggs are cooked as you like them. Serve at once.

Version 2

> 1 oz (30 g) butter
> 1 large onion, finely chopped
> 4 rashers bacon, cut in fine strips
> 6 oz (180 g) mushrooms, finely sliced

Melt the butter and fry the onion until soft and just beginning to brown. Push to one side of the pan and fry the bacon and mushrooms, turning and stirring all the time. Set aside to keep warm. Remove the potatoes from the oven and cut evenly in halves lengthways. Scoop out half a tablespoon of the inside from each half. Pile the fried mixture into the bottom halves, shut down the tops lightly, and return to the oven for 5 minutes. Serve immediately.

Version 3

> 2 oz (60 g) butter
> 2 oz (60 g) milk
> 2 tablespoons fresh parsley, finely chopped
> pinch finely chopped thyme
> pinch garlic salt (if liked)
> salt and pepper

Cut the baked potatoes in halves lengthways, and scoop out all the insides, being careful not to break the skins. Heat the butter and milk in a saucepan until the butter is just melting and stir in all the potato. Beat for a moment above but not directly on the heat, and then stir in the herbs and seasoning. Put back into the potatoes, closing the halves together, and return to the oven for 10 minutes before serving.

Surprise Tomatoes

For this dish, very large tomatoes are required (the Mediterranean type are best of all), as each has to contain an egg. Brown bread and butter and a green salad are very good with these tomatoes.

For 4
4 very large tomatoes
salt, pepper and sugar
4 eggs (not too large)
2 oz (60 g) mushrooms, finely chopped and lightly
    sautéed in butter
2 oz (60 g) butter
2 oz (60 g) finely grated cheese
1 tablespoon finely chopped parsley

Cut the top off each tomato and set aside. Scoop out all the seeds and juice with a teaspoon, being very careful not to break the skin. (The pulp and juice can be strained and kept for soup or a sauce.) Sprinkle the insides of the tomatoes with a very little salt, pepper and sugar. Break an egg into each and sprinkle with a little salt. Put a spoonful of chopped sautéed mushrooms and a small piece of butter on each. Replace the tops of the tomatoes. Carefully stand them in a well-buttered, shallow fireproof dish, and bake in a pre-heated oven at 350°F, gas mark 4, for 10 minutes. Remove from the oven and sprinkle each tomato quite thickly with cheese. Spoon the juice and butter over and return to the oven for a further 3 minutes. Serve immediately, sprinkling each with parsley. The eggs should be soft but set.

11. Vegetables as Accompaniments

The unhappy phrase 'meat and two veg' still haunts the foreigner's conception of English cooking and English menus. It is a phrase which belonged to cheap lodgings and landladies' cooking and which has nothing to do with the food of today. Or has it? Are we still apt to serve potatoes and a plain boiled green vegetable or carrots and feel that duty is done?

The collection of recipes which follow suggest slightly more elaborate and unusual, and much more interesting, cooking of vegetables. Simple grilled chops or joints of chicken, for instance, are elevated to an outstanding supper dish if Brussels Sprouts with Green Grapes, Cauliflower in the Polish Manner or Dauphinois Potatoes and a green salad are served with them. Pot Herbs in Gravy is enough in itself without additional meat, as long as the gravy is good, but is also excellent served with sausages or cutlets.

Brussels Sprouts with Chestnuts

This is very good with any roast or bird and with cold ham or any cold salad.

For 4   1 lb (½ kg) Brussels sprouts, stalks and outer
              leaves trimmed
              1½ oz (45 g) butter
              8 oz (240 g) cooked and skinned chestnuts
              seasoning

Put the sprouts into boiling salted water just to cover, and boil until just tender (approx. 20 minutes). Melt the butter in a pan and heat without allowing to brown. Fry the chestnuts in it for 2 minutes, turning and breaking them up into pieces. Add the sprouts and toss with the chestnuts for a further 2 minutes. Mix lightly together and season, then turn on to a hot dish and serve.

Brussels Sprouts with Green Grapes

This is delicious served in individual dishes as a hot hors d'oeuvre, with fried croûtons to eat with it. It is also a perfect vegetable to serve with any roast bird, particularly game birds, and is very good with veal in any form.

For 4   1 lb (½ kg) small, firm sprouts
            8 oz (240 g) green grapes
            1 oz (30 g) butter

Put the sprouts into boiling salted water just to cover and boil for approximately 15 minutes. While they are cooking, blanch and seed the grapes. Drain the sprouts when cooked and toss in the butter for 2 minutes. Lightly mix in the grapes, turn on to a hot serving dish, and serve at once, very hot.

Cabbage with Caraway Seeds

The very strong and distinctive flavour of caraway seeds is not liked by everyone. However, it seems to bring out the flavour of winter white cabbage, and if you do like the seeds, this dish served with sausages or gammon rashers makes an excellent supper.

For 4   1½ lb (¾ kg) white cabbage
            ½ teaspoon salt
            ½ teaspoon ground nutmeg
            1 teaspoon caraway seeds
            1 onion, peeled and chopped
            ¾ pint (4½ dl) chicken stock
            ½ oz (15 g) butter
            ½ teaspoon pepper

Wash the cabbage well, shred it finely and place in a large saucepan with the salt, nutmeg, caraway seeds, onion and stock. Bring to the boil and allow to simmer for 30–40 minutes. Strain and add the butter and pepper. Toss well and serve very hot.

Carrots Vichy

For 4   2 lb (1 kg) carrots
            2 oz (60 g) butter

                salt and pepper
                a little sugar
                1 rasher bacon, chopped
                1 tablespoon chopped parsley

Scrape the carrots and cut into slices. Melt 1½ oz (45 g) of butter in a saucepan and toss the sliced carrots in it for a few minutes. Cover with water, season with salt, pepper and a little sugar, and add the chopped rasher of bacon. Simmer gently for 25 minutes, until the carrots are tender. The liquid should have almost evaporated – do not drain, as what is left will have become a good sauce: stir in the remaining ½ oz (15 g) of butter, pour the whole into a hot serving dish, sprinkle with chopped parsley and serve very hot.

Cauliflower in the Polish Manner

For 4   1 large cauliflower or two smaller
                4 hard-boiled eggs, very finely chopped
                1 tablespoon parsley, finely chopped
                juice of ½ lemon
                salt and pepper
                2 oz (60 g) butter, melted and allowed to become
                    light brown (but not burnt)

Boil the cauliflower till just tender but not soft. Drain and place on a heated dish. Divide it into four (or each into halves, if two are used). Sprinkle the chopped eggs all over, and the parsley over the eggs. Pour over the lemon juice and a little salt and pepper. Finally, pour over the butter and serve at once. If it is to be a main dish, serve it with a savoury toast for each person (see p. 131).

Champignons à la Grecque

Traditional as a starting course in Greece. Serve with crusty brown bread, which is usually dipped in the juice.

For 4   12 oz (360 g) small button mushrooms, or larger
                    mushrooms, sliced, stalk and all
                ½ gill cooking oil (sunflower or walnut oil are best –
                    olive oil would be used in Greece, but is heavier)
                juice of ½ lemon
                ½ gill white wine

       1 clove garlic, crushed
       1 bay leaf
       1 stalk celery
       1 sprig thyme
       1 sprig rosemary
       6 peppercorns
       salt

Simmer all the ingredients very gently together for 15 minutes. Allow to cool, covered, then remove the thyme, bay leaf, rosemary and celery stalk, and serve the mushrooms cold in the liquid in which they cooked.

Grandmother's Peas with Bacon

For 4   2 lb (1 kg) peas
       2 rashers lean bacon, cut in fine strips
       1 oz (30 g) butter
       1 medium onion *or* 2 shallots, chopped finely
       1 teaspoon sugar
       1 teaspoon salt
       1 lettuce leaf
       a little chopped mint and parsley

Shell the peas. Fry the bacon in a saucepan, add the butter and the chopped onion and fry for another minute. Put in the peas and shake the pan so that they are coated with the butter. Add 1 teaspoon each of sugar and salt. Put in the lettuce leaf, and add ¼ pint (1½ dl) of boiling water. Cover the pan closely and cook for 15 minutes, stirring from time to time, and adding a little more water if it is all absorbed. When the peas are tender, serve without draining, sprinkled with chopped mint and parsley.

A Supper Dish of Green Peas

For 4   2 lb (1 kg) peas
       2 rashers lean bacon, cut in fine strips
       1 oz (30 g) butter
       1 medium onion *or* 2 shallots, chopped finely
       1 teaspoon sugar
       1 teaspoon salt

1 lettuce leaf
a little chopped mint and parsley
4 chipolata sausages
12 very small cooked new potatoes

Proceed exactly as above, but add 4 chipolata sausages cut in rings and fried and a dozen very small cooked new potatoes to the peas 3 or 4 minutes before they are cooked. Pour into a fireproof dish and serve as a luncheon or supper dish, with triangles of fried bread.

Potatoes Anna

For 4   2 lb (1 kg) potatoes
8 oz (240 g) butter
seasoning

Wash and peel the potatoes and slice into thin, even slices. Butter a round fireproof mould well, and put a layer of potatoes at the bottom, spreading them evenly. Season with pepper and salt. Melt the rest of the butter and pour a little over the potatoes. Then add another layer of potatoes, more butter and seasoning, and continue until the mould is nearly full. Put the mould into a hot oven, 450°F, gas mark 8, and bake for 1 hour. Turn the mould upside down on a plate to drain. Remove the mould and the potatoes will be light brown and hold the shape of the mould.

Baked Potatoes with Mustard

These potatoes are intended to be served with slices of cold beef or ham, or good Cheddar, Sage Derby or Leicester cheese, and a dressed green salad to which two or three eating apples, peeled, cored and finely sliced, are added. Cox's are best of all for this. The mustard enhances the flavour of the beef, ham or cheese and the salad contrasts and refreshes. A perfect autumn supper with red wine or beer.

For 4   4 large potatoes of roughly even size
3 oz (90 g) butter (soft but not melted)
1 tablespoon double cream
1 tablespoon made mustard
½ teaspoon French mustard
salt and pepper

Scrub the potatoes, removing any eyes and blemishes, and pierce each twice with a skewer. Lightly rub the skins over with some of the butter. Place in a baking tray and bake at 350°F, gas mark 4, for 1½ hours. Meanwhile, beat the remaining butter with the cream and mustards to form a smooth, fairly thick cream. Divide into 4 pats and chill for at least half an hour. Just before the meal is to be served, take the potatoes from the oven and cut them horizontally with a sharp knife so that the halves are joined only by a hinge. Sprinkle the cut sides with salt and pepper and close. Slip a pat of the chilled mustard cream into each and serve. Transfer them quickly to each person's plate so that he or she can open the potato out flat and mash the mustard cream into each half before it is too much melted.

Dauphinois Potatoes

For 4
2 lb (1 kg) potatoes
salt and pepper
a little butter
2 oz (60 g) grated cheese
1 egg
½ pint (3 dl) milk

Peel the potatoes, slice them finely, and sprinkle them with salt and pepper. Take an earthenware casserole, butter it well, and place a thin layer of sliced potatoes in it. Sprinkle with some of the grated cheese, then cover with another layer of potatoes sprinkled with cheese, and continue in alternate layers until the casserole is full. Mix the beaten egg with the milk and pour this mixture over the potatoes. Dot with butter, cover tightly, and cook very slowly in a moderate oven, about 350°F, gas mark 4, for 30–40 minutes. Uncover and cook for a further 10 minutes near the top of the oven so that the top may brown.

Duchesse Potatoes

2 lb (1 kg) potatoes
2 oz (60 g) butter
¼ pint (1½ dl) milk
2 eggs

Cook the potatoes in boiling salted water, drain, and put through a fine sieve or moulin. Heat the butter and milk in a saucepan, add the sieved potato, and stir until it is hot and creamy. Remove from the heat, add the eggs (unbeaten), and whip well with an egg-beater or wire whisk. Butter a flat oven tray well and place the potato mixture on the tray in tablespoonfuls, or pipe it into éclair shapes. Put into a moderate oven, about 350°F, gas mark 4, for 20 minutes, or until the separate shapes are golden brown and beginning to crisp.

Pot Herbs in Gravy

Carrots, turnips, onions, swedes and parsnips were called 'pot herbs' because they were always put in the large iron pot which hung over the open fire in farms and cottages when any meat or bird was being stewed. If meat was short, the children were often served only the vegetables and gravy.

Pot herbs, which should not be very large or tough, but need not be very young, specially cooked in good meat stock, make a delicious and good-looking dish served with creamed potato and very green cabbage or peas.

For 4   1 lb (½ kg) carrots
              1 lb (½ kg) young turnips
              1 lb (½ kg) onions (4–6 to the lb)
              1 lb (½ kg) parsnips or swedes (if liked; if not used,
                 prepare 1½ lb (¾ kg) each carrots and turnips)
              1½ pints (9 dl) very good brown stock
              seasoning
              1½ oz (45 g) butter
              1½ oz (45 g) flour
              1 small glass sherry or 1 tablespoon brandy (optional)
              1 tablespoon chopped parsley

Peel all the vegetables. Cut the carrots in rounds about ¾ inch (1½ cm) thick, and the turnips in slices ½ inch (1 cm) thick, cut in half across. Quarter the onions and cut the parsnips or swedes like the carrots.

Put all the vegetables in a casserole and cover with the stock. Season well with salt and pepper, bring to the boil, and simmer gently, covered, either in the oven or on top of the stove for 2 hours. Check that all the vegetables are tender. Lift them from the stock on to a warmed shallow dish, using a pierced spoon or slice, and keep warm. Thicken the stock with a roux of the butter and flour. It should be the consistency of single cream. If it is not a good brown, add a little soy or gravy browning. Check the seasoning. A small glass of sherry or a tablespoon of cooking brandy will enrich it but is not essential. Pour the sauce over the pot herbs, sprinkle with parsley and serve.

A Winter Supper of Red Cabbage with Chestnuts

This dish comes from Kent. The sixteenth-century manuscript says that it was served with the Michaelmas goose. It is excellent with roast lamb or with grilled lamb or pork chops.

For 6
1½ lb (¾ kg) chestnuts
3 oz (90 g) butter or 3 tablespoons cooking oil
2 large onions, peeled and thinly sliced
1 red cabbage, about 3lb (1½ kg) in weight, stalk removed and finely shredded
8 oz (240 g) large prunes, soaked, stoned and coarsely chopped
1 large cooking apple, peeled, cored, quartered and sliced
salt and freshly ground black pepper
¼ pint (1½ dl) red wine

Make a hole in each chestnut with a skewer, place them on a dry baking tin, and put them in the oven preheated to 250°F, gas mark 1, for 20 minutes. Take the chestnuts from the oven, cool for a minute and then peel them, keeping them as whole as possible, digging out any fragments so that none are wasted. Heat the butter or oil in a large fireproof casserole and when hot stir in the onions, cooking gently until they are transparent but not brown.

Stir in half the cabbage, the chestnuts, prunes and apple. Mix well, add the remaining cabbage and mix again. Stir in salt and pepper and pour in the wine. Cover closely with foil and cook for 1½–2 hours at 350°F, gas mark 4. Make sure the cabbage is tender, check the seasoning and serve.

12. Salads

All through the long English winters poor men thought of the pleasures of spring and summer. It would be warmer, daylight would come earlier and darkness fall later, and there would be fresh foods instead of salted and dried. Only the well-to-do kept a few sheep and cows through the winter for fresh meat for their households, and even they could not provide fresh vegetables. So the first young green leaves and shoots that could be eaten as salad were sought with passion in the fields and hedgerows as soon as April brought a few warm days. Wild 'saladings' came sooner than cultivated ones and cost nothing. The poor family probably ate a bowl of young dandelion leaves, hawthorn buds and the first leaves of sorrel, dressed with last autumn's home-made vinegar since both oil and salt were often too expensive, served with barley bread or oat cakes. At the manor house the first parsley and some young onions might be added, and the salad dressed with plenty of oil and vinegar, salt, and sometimes a scraping of sugar.

Nettle shoots were gathered, washed, and cooked to be served as a 'boiled salad'. By early summer, many species of herbs were gathered from both manor and cottage garden, flowers and fruit were added, and, in wealthy houses, 'compound' salads of great elaboration were placed as side dishes or centre pieces for the first course of princely feasts. Well dressed with oil and vinegar, these were 'always eaten with delight'.

Individual Apple Salads

These salads are particularly good with cold pork or duck or chicken, but are also very good for lunch or supper served with stuffed baked potatoes.

For 4   4 large Cox's Orange Pippins
           a little lemon juice
           1 green pepper, de-seeded and very finely chopped

2 sticks of celery, strings removed and very finely
chopped
1 tablespoon chives, finely chopped
1 tablespoon parsley, finely chopped
3 tablespoons mayonnaise
1 lettuce
1 bunch watercress
2 tablespoons French dressing
2 oz (60 g) walnuts, shelled and chopped (reserve 4
halves)

Remove the stems from the apples and with a small, sharp knife cut a slice from the top of each. Cut round inside the skins, being careful not to pierce them, and scoop out the cores and as much pulp as possible. There should be only a thin layer of pulp left inside the skin. Squeeze a little lemon juice over the inside of each apple, to prevent discolouring. Slice and chop all the apple pulp, apart from the cores, and mix it with the green pepper, celery, chives and parsley. Finally stir in the mayonnaise, and fill each apple with the mixture.

Remove the outside leaves and stalk of the lettuce and the stalks of the watercress. Break any large lettuce leaves into pieces, mix the lettuce and watercress, and pour the French dressing over them, mixing it lightly.

Put a quarter of this salad on each of four small plates, and stand an apple in the centre of each green bed. Sprinkle the walnuts over the salad around the apples, and put a half walnut in the centre of each apple.

Five Bean Salad

This is a splendid salad for a summer lunch party. It is French in origin, and should accompany a large flat dish of carefully arranged slices of ham, tongue, chicken or turkey, and two or more kinds of sliced sausage. Navy beans, black-eyed beans, etc., can replace the butter or red beans if preferred or more easily obtainable. Dried thyme and marjoram can be used.

For 8   8 oz (240 g) haricot beans, soaked overnight, boiled
till tender in salted water (about 2 hours) and
allowed to get cold

8 oz (240 g) red beans, cooked as haricot beans

8 oz (240 g) butter beans, cooked as haricot beans

8 oz (240 g) fresh or frozen broad beans, cooked and
cooled

1 lb (½ kg) French beans, ends and strings removed
and cooked whole until just tender

3 tablespoons finely chopped fresh parsley

½ tablespoon finely chopped thyme

½ tablespoon finely chopped marjoram

8 oz (240 g) shallots or salad onions, skinned and very
finely chopped

3 cloves garlic, skinned and finely chopped, unless
not liked

½ pint (3 dl) good French dressing into which a full
teaspoon of French mustard has been stirred until
dissolved

Reserve 12 of the French beans for decoration.

Put a little of the dressing in the bottom of a large bowl (a mixing
bowl is suitable). Lightly mix in some of each kind of bean, and
sprinkle with a little parsley and a pinch of thyme and marjoram.
Sprinkle with chopped shallots and season.

Add another layer of beans, herbs, shallots and seasoning, and
then some more dressing. Always mix very lightly, and repeat the
layers till all the ingredients are in the bowl. Sprinkle the top with
the remaining parsley, and lay the reserved French beans in a lattice
over it.

Céléri Rémoulade

For 4   1 lb (½ kg) celery or celeriac

1 gill lemon juice

2 tablespoons mustard

½ teaspoon sugar

salt and pepper

about ¼ pint (1½ dl) olive oil

1 egg yolk

2 tablespoons cream

few drops wine or tarragon vinegar

Peel, slice thinly and shred or grate the celery or celeriac. Mix it with the lemon juice to keep it white. Place the mustard, sugar, salt and pepper in a basin and whisk vigorously while adding the olive oil. When the sauce begins to thicken, add the egg yolk and continue whisking. Finally, mix in the cream and vinegar. Stir the sauce into the celery, and allow it to stand for 1 hour before serving.

Individual Chicken Salads with Hot Potatoes

Very good for summer lunches or suppers, and easy to make and serve for a party. The lettuce must be very crisp and the herbs fresh. The very small hot potatoes make an interesting contrast with the chilled salad.

For 8
8 chicken joints, roasted and allowed to get cold
1 cucumber, peeled and cut into ½ inch (1 cm) cubes
3 oz (90 g) green olives, stoned and chopped
1 tablespoon chopped fennel
2 tablespoons chopped parsley
2 tablespoons chopped mint
2 tablespoons chopped chives
salt and freshly ground black pepper
4 small (5 oz/150 g) cartons natural yoghurt
¼ pint (1½ dl) double cream
3 lb (1½ kg) small new potatoes, scraped
1 oz (30 g) butter
2 Webb's or Iceberg lettuces

Strip all the white meat and the best of the dark meat from the chicken joints, reserving the skin and bones to make stock for another occasion. Chop the chicken meat into ½ inch (1 cm) pieces. Add the chopped cucumber, the olives, fennel, half the parsley, half the mint and half the chives. Season lightly with salt and fairly heavily with freshly ground black pepper. Pour in the yoghurt and the cream and mix all well together. Refrigerate for 2 hours or longer. Half an hour before the dish is to be served, put the new potatoes into boiling salted water and boil for 15–20 minutes. Drain well, toss in butter and keep hot.

Remove the outside leaves from the lettuces, reserving eight good ones, cut the hard centres in quarters and then cut across. Wash, shake, dry and put two heart pieces and one leaf on each plate. Fill the leaves with the chilled chicken mixture and sprinkle with the remaining parsley and chives. Put 2 or 3 hot potatoes between the lettuce hearts, not touching them, on each plate, and sprinkle with the remaining mint. Serve immediately.

Salads of Eggs and Walnuts

These distinguished salads make a complete light meal. Serve in individual dishes with plenty of thin brown bread and butter. Very good with a rough, red wine. For a sumptuous supper, follow with a chocolate cake accompanied by a glass of Scotch or Irish coffee.

For 4   1 Webb's or Iceberg lettuce
¼ pint (1½ dl) mayonnaise (home-made is best, but any good make will do)
4 hard-boiled eggs
salt and freshly ground black pepper
4 oz (120 g) chopped walnuts
12 walnut halves

Wash the lettuce, removing the outside leaves, and chop finely. Mix with a little mayonnaise and divide among the four bowls. Chop the eggs finely, season lightly, and mix with some more mayonnaise. Season the chopped walnuts with a little salt and plenty of pepper. Put a thin layer of walnuts on the lettuce, then a layer of the egg mixture, then more walnuts until all are used, ending with walnuts. Decorate each bowl with 3 walnut halves. Place in the refrigerator for a few minutes (but not more than an hour) before serving.

Kentish Salad

From the Middle Ages to the early part of this century, Kent was famous for its hazel nuts, sold in all the big markets as Kentish cobs. The soil of the Weald of Kent suited the nut trees, which were pruned to grow in the shape of great urns. At Canterbury there was a particularly famous orchard, where the frilled, pale green clusters showed bright against the heavy dark green leaves from September to October, and children were employed to drive off the squirrels. This is a very fine winter salad and can be made with ready-shelled hazel nuts.

For 4   8 oz (240 g) shelled hazel nuts, roughly chopped
2 oz (60 g) raisins, soaked in hot water for half an hour and drained

2 Cox's Orange Pippins, peeled, cored and finely
  sliced
8 oz (240 g) finely grated white cabbage
6 sticks celery, strings removed and finely chopped
½ medium onion, skinned and very finely chopped
1 clove garlic, crushed
2 oz (60 g) home-made or any good mayonnaise,
  mixed with 1 tablespoon double cream
½ teaspoon powdered mace

Mix the nuts, fruit, vegetables and garlic together in a large bowl.
Stir the mace into the mayonnaise, pour over the vegetables, and
mix lightly so that everything is evenly coated.

Lettuce Salad with Peas in Aspic

Very good as a light luncheon dish or to accompany grilled trout or
lamb cutlets.

For 4   1 packet of aspic jelly to make 1 pint (6 dl)
               1 tablespoon mint and parsley, finely chopped
                 together
               2 hard-boiled eggs, finely chopped
               8 oz (240 g) green peas, shelled and cooked, fresh or
                 frozen
               1 hard lettuce
               2 tablespoons French dressing
               1 tablespoon double cream
               2 oz (60 g) Philadelphia cream cheese

Make up the aspic jelly according to directions. Cool and put in the
refrigerator till just beginning to set (about 30 minutes). Meanwhile
take four individual soufflé dishes, or any 4 oz (120 g) cups or bowls,
and put a little of the chopped mint and parsley in the bottom of
each. Put a quarter of the chopped eggs on top, and a quarter of the
peas on top of the egg. As soon as the jelly is just starting to set,
spoon a little into each dish. The layers should not be quite covered.
Put the dishes in the refrigerator to set firmly, but keep the
remaining jelly in a cool place to avoid firm setting. When the
moulds are firmly set, take out of the refrigerator and fill up with
more layers of chopped egg and peas and then jelly. Put any
remaining jelly and the filled moulds back into the refrigerator to

set firm. All the above may be done on the day before the salads are required if more convenient.

A few minutes before they are to be served, chop the lettuce very finely, dress lightly with French dressing and arrange on a large flat dish. Turn the moulds out one at a time on to a plate, and slide each on to the bed of lettuce. (If the jellies stick in the moulds, pull gently away from the sides and try again. If they still stick, stand for a few seconds in half an inch of very hot water. If too hot, or if they are left too long, the tops begin to melt). Chop any jelly left over with a knife and put small piles between the moulds. Stir the cream and cream cheese together and place a spoonful on each mould. Sprinkle with the remaining mint and parsley and serve. If the salad is to accompany fish or meat served on hot plates, small cold plates must be provided for each person.

Salad Niçoise

For 4   1 lettuce
              4 tomatoes
              2 hard-boiled eggs
              4 oz (120 g) black olives
              4 oz (120 g) anchovy fillets, each cut in half
              1 clove garlic
              French dressing
              1 large tin tuna fish
              thyme

Wash, dry and finely shred the lettuce. Blanch and chop the tomatoes, shell and chop the eggs and mix together with the lettuce in a large bowl. Stone the olives and mix them in, together with the anchovy fillets. Crush one clove of garlic into the dressing, pour it over the salad, pile the tuna fish into the centre, sprinkle with chopped thyme, and serve.

Orange and Watercress Salad with Raisins

Very good with duck or pheasant or served alone as a starting course. The orange must be sweet.

For 4   3 bunches of watercress
              3 oz (90 g) seedless raisins
              4 large oranges
              juice of ½ lemon

½ teaspoon sugar
½ teaspoon salt
½ teaspoon pepper
2 tablespoons olive oil

Wash the watercress well, cut off any hard stalks and roughly chop the remainder. Pour a little boiling water over the raisins and leave to soak for a few minutes. Peel 3 of the oranges, scrape clean of pith, and cut across in very thin slices with a sharp knife. Remove any pips with the point of the knife.

Squeeze the remaining orange and strain the juice into a small jug or bowl. Stir in the lemon juice, sugar, salt and pepper and mix well. Pour in the olive oil, a little at a time, always stirring. Finish the dressing by beating with a fork or electric beater. The orange juice and the oil should be integrated to the consistency of a thin cream.

Arrange the watercress to cover a flat dish and pour the dressing all over it, working the watercress into it a little with a fork. Lay the orange slices on it, working outwards from the middle and arranging them to overlap slightly. Drain the raisins and dry gently with kitchen paper. Sprinkle over the orange slices. Chill for about 15 minutes in the refrigerator before serving.

The Best Rice Salad in the World

This salad was traditionally served in the South of France in the full heat of summer. It was made in a huge bowl to serve eight or ten people at lunch or supper on the terrace, with no accompaniments but good bread and rough wine.

For 6
2 large green peppers
2 large red peppers
4 or 5 large tomatoes
1 clove garlic, well crushed
4 oz (120 g) grapes, white or black, blanched, skinned and stoned
4 oz (120 g) black olives, stoned and chopped
2 oz (60 g) walnuts, roughly chopped
4 oz (120 g) sultanas, soaked in hot water for 30 minutes and drained
2 teaspoons finely chopped rosemary and thyme

4 oz (120 g) long grain or brown rice, cooked till just
    tender and allowed to become quite cold
salt and fresh black pepper
juice 2 large or 3 smaller lemons
½ pint (3 dl) double cream

Halve the peppers and remove the seeds. Place with the cut side
down in a hot oven for 5 minutes, then remove as much skin as
possible and cut the flesh in ¼ inch (½ cm) strips. Slice the tomatoes
thinly, without skinning, and mix with the crushed garlic.

Mix all the ingredients except the cream and lemon juice lightly
together, and season rather highly with salt and pepper. Chill for an
hour or two or for longer. When just about to serve, pour the lemon
juice over and lightly mix it in, and immediately after pour over and
mix in the cream. Serve immediately.

Salamagundy

This is a very ancient dish, dating back to medieval and possibly to
Roman-British times. Recipes vary through the centuries, but it is
very like a dish described in the only existing Roman cookery book,
which was put together by Apicius.

To make this dish for a lunch or supper party is a labour of love,
and should not be undertaken by anyone with limited time and
energy. It is a dish to be enjoyed in the making.

A Salamagundy (the name was often spelt Salamongundy) was
an elaborate salad which had to be both delicious to eat and
extremely ornamental. It was usually laid out in one of two ways.
Either the finely shredded ingredients were arranged in rings on
a very large platter with a bowl set upside down in the centre,
the rings were continued over this bowl and on the top a figure
modelled in butter was placed, often surrounded by very green
and curly parsley with nasturtiums or marigold petals set among
it. Or the different ingredients were piled in small saucers or
silver dishes set in a circle on a large platter, in the centre of
which was a raised comport or ham dish. Parsley was arranged
between all the saucers and an ornament of butter set among
flowers on the comport. At least eight or ten different ingredients
were considered appropriate for this salad, including chicken and
anchovies.

For 6–8   2 large, crisp Webb's or Iceberg lettuces
2 tablespoons watercress, stalks removed and leaves
  well washed
1 cucumber, peeled, de-seeded and cut into ½ inch
  (1 cm) cubes
16 small onions, peeled and cooked, or tinned, or
  frozen and defrosted
1 lb (480 g) tomatoes (yellow ones look and taste well
  in this salad), blanched and cut in quarters
6 hard-boiled eggs, yolks and whites separated
2 tablespoons finely chopped parsley
8 oz (240 g) cooked white meat of chicken, cut into
  strips about 2 inches (4 cm) long and ½ inch (1 cm)
  wide
8 oz (240 g) dark meat of chicken cut in the same way
2 tins anchovy fillets, drained
20 black olives, stoned and halved
12 nasturtium flowers, or a tablespoon of marigold
  petals or yellow rose petals (the colour was
  important and all these flowers were considered
  edible)
8 oz (240 g) cooked whole French beans, each cut in
  two
8 oz (240 g) green grapes, stoned and blanched
½ pint (3 dl) French dressing
seasoning

Shred the lettuce very finely and evenly, and arrange in a layer all over a large platter. Around the edge arrange a circle of watercress. Next to it, working inwards, arrange a circle of cucumber mixed with the small onions. Next to this arrange the tomatoes in a circle, sprinkling them with the chopped egg whites and half the chopped parsley. Next to them arrange a circle of the white chicken meat. Mash the egg yolks, or put them through a blender, and mix into them the dark chicken meat and half the drained anchovy fillets, each cut in four. Season with a little black pepper and stir in the remaining parsley. Pile on top of and up the sides of an inverted bowl in the middle of the platter. Make a ring of black olives round the central mixture. Stand the remaining anchovy fillets up the central mound. On top of the mound arrange the flower heads or petals. Put the French beans and the grapes separately wherever there is a space, or where their colours contrast with another ingredient. Spoon the French dressing round each ring of the salad just before serving.

Serving spoons should be laid round the great dish so that each person can help himself without hurry to as many of the ingredients as he fancies.

Supreme Salad

This is the King of Salads. It requires no accompaniments for Sunday lunch or supper on a fine summer's day. It takes quite a long time to buy, prepare and assemble the ingredients, and is best made when there is time for this to be a pleasure. A very large meat dish or a tray covered in silver foil will be required. Serve with French bread and unsalted butter, and a dry white wine.

For 6
8 oz (240 g) Philadephia cream cheese
2 oz (60 g) double cream
¼ teaspoon powdered turmeric
1 teaspoon French mustard
12 oz (360 g) cooked chicken, boneless and neatly diced
6 oz (180 g) firm button mushrooms, very finely sliced
3 hard-boiled eggs
3 oz (90 g) walnuts, finely chopped
2 crisp Webb's or Iceberg lettuces
1 small, ripe, fresh pineapple
8 oz (240 g) chicory
8 oz (240 g) French beans, cooked till just tender
60 crisp croûtons of fried bread, each ½ inch (1 cm) square
1 teaspoon fresh thyme, finely chopped
1 tablespoon fresh parsley, finely chopped
French dressing
6 oz (180 g) home-made or Hellmann's mayonnaise

Mix the cream cheese with the double cream and beat for a minute with a fork. Stir in the turmeric and the French mustard and beat again. Lightly fold in the chicken and the mushrooms. Chop the hard-boiled eggs finely in a separate bowl and mix them with the walnuts.

Prepare the lettuces by removing the outer leaves and hard stalks, and then shred in a machine or very carefully by hand, so that the ribbons of lettuce are about ⅛–¼ inch (¼–½ cm) wide. Make a bed of lettuce over the dish or tray, piling it higher round the sides and ends. Peel and core the pineapple, slice it, and cut each slice in four. Arrange these pieces on the lettuce border.

Next arrange the chicory, separating the leaves and leaning them up against the outer wall. Arrange the French beans against the chicory. Pile the chicken mixture in the middle of the dish. Round the pile and partly on the French beans, put spoonfuls of the walnut and egg mixture. Sprinkle the croûtons over the walnuts and egg.

Sprinkle the thyme over the chicken and the parsley over the lettuce and pineapple. Serve at once, or keep in the refrigerator for not more than an hour. French dressing and mayonnaise should be offered separately.

A Wild Salad Today

Anyone who lives or even spends a day in the country can gather a wild salad which will be a revelation. The best months are April and May. All leaves must be young and new; those which, on certain plants, have survived the winter are tough and bitter.

The basis of such a salad today is generally young dandelion leaves, which can be found almost anywhere, even on waste ground in cities. Pick about 20 for each person. Sorrel should just be shooting, and about 12 of its small leaves, sourer than the dandelion leaves, gives a good proportion. Naturally, the variety of plants available depends on the district. New leaves of wild violets, 2 or 3 per person, are good. Wild garlic is found in many districts, and 2 or 3 leaves and stems can be added. If tiny shoots of wild thyme can be found, they will give the salad real distinction. A small handful of hawthorn leaf buds, still very small, which children used to call bread and cheese, give a slightly nutty flavour. If watercress is available, add a dozen sprigs for each person, which increases the bulk of the salad. The first tiny shoots of bugloss can be added, and buds from the broom. Add a few young wild strawberry leaves, a very few leaves of woodsorrel (which is very sharp in taste), and leaves of wild peppermint, if they can be found.

It is important, today, to be very careful not to destroy any wild plant but only to take one or two leaves or shoots gently from each single plant.

If you take home a double handful of leaves and shoots, even if only dandelion and sorrel, and wash them well, shake them in a cloth and dress them with a dressing of oil, wine vinegar and a little sugar, salt and pepper, you will have a small amount of salad for each person, tender and delicate, but with a strong, refreshing taste, and you will be eating exactly what our ancestors ate in the spring seasons of 500 years ago.

Index

MORE ABOUT PENGUINS, PELICANS
AND PUFFINS

For further information about books available from Penguins please write to Dept EP, Penguin Books Ltd, Harmondsworth, Middlesex UB7 ODA.

In the U.S.A.: For a complete list of books available from Penguins in the United States write to Dept DG, Penguin Books, 299 Murray Hill Parkway, East Rutherford, New Jersey 07073.

In Canada: For a complete list of books available from Penguins in Canada write to Penguin Books Canada Ltd, 2801 John Street, Markham, Ontario L3R 1B4.

In Australia: For a complete list of books available from Penguins in Australia write to the Marketing Department, Penguin Books Australia Ltd, P.O. Box 257, Ringwood, Victoria 3134.

In New Zealand: For a complete list of books available from Penguins in New Zealand write to the Marketing Department, Penguin Books (N.Z.) Ltd, P.O. Box 4019, Auckland 10.

In India: For a complete list of books available from Penguins in India write to Penguin Overseas Ltd, 706 Eros Apartments, 56 Nehru Place, New Delhi 110019.